# Trump
## First Week Remarks

West Martian Limited Company
1st Edition, January 2025

First printing 2025
The publisher can be contacted at westmartian.com
ISBN-13: 979-8-3484-8794-2 Paperback

# Contents

# Trump
## First Week Remarks

# Remarks

## The Inaugural Address

### January 20, 2025 12:10 P.M. EST

U.S. Capitol Washington, D.C.

THE PRESIDENT: Thank you. Thank you very much, everybody. (Applause.) Wow. Thank you very, very much.

Vice President Vance, Speaker Johnson, Senator Thune, Chief Justice Roberts, justices of the Supreme Court of the United States, President Clinton, President Bush, President Obama, President Biden, Vice President Harris, and my fellow citizens, the golden age of America begins right now. (Applause.)

From this day forward, our country will flourish and be respected again all over the world. We will be the envy of every nation, and we will not allow ourselves to be taken advantage of any longer. During every single day of the Trump administration, I will, very simply, put America first. (Applause.)

Our sovereignty will be reclaimed. Our safety will be restored. The scales of justice will be rebalanced. The vicious, violent, and unfair weaponization of the Justice Department and our government will end. (Applause.)

And our top priority will be to create a nation that is proud, prosperous, and free. (Applause.)

America will soon be greater, stronger, and far more exceptional than ever before. (Applause.)

I return to the presidency confident and optimistic that we are at the start of a thrilling new era of national success. A tide of change is sweeping the country, sunlight is pouring over the entire world, and America has the chance to seize this opportunity like never before.

But first, we must be honest about the challenges we face. While they are plentiful, they will be annihilated by this great momentum that the world is now witnessing in the United States of America.

As we gather today, our government confronts a crisis of trust. For many years, a radical and corrupt establishment has extracted power and wealth from our citizens while the pillars of our society lay broken and seemingly in complete disrepair.

We now have a government that cannot manage even a simple crisis at home while, at the same time, stumbling into a continuing catalogue of catastrophic events abroad.

It fails to protect our magnificent, law-abiding American citizens but provides sanctuary and protection for dangerous criminals, many from prisons and mental institutions, that have illegally entered our country from all over the world.

We have a government that has given unlimited funding to the defense of foreign borders but refuses to defend American borders or, more importantly, its own people.

Our country can no longer deliver basic services in times of emergency, as recently shown by the wonderful people of North Carolina — who have been treated so badly — (applause) — and other states who are still suffering from a hurricane that took place many months ago or, more recently, Los Angeles, where we are watching fires still tragically burn from weeks ago without even a token of defense. They're raging through the houses and communities, even affecting some of the wealthiest and most powerful individuals in our country — some of whom are sitting here right now. They don't have a home any longer. That's interesting. But we can't let this happen. Everyone is unable to do anything about it. That's going to change.

We have a public health system that does not deliver in times of disaster, yet more money is spent on it than any country anywhere in the world.

And we have an education system that teaches our children to be ashamed of themselves — in many cases, to hate our country despite the love that we try so desperately to provide to them. All of this will change starting today, and it will change very quickly. (Applause.)

My recent election is a mandate to completely and totally reverse a horrible betrayal and all of these many betrayals that have taken place and to give the people back their faith, their wealth, their democracy, and, indeed, their freedom. From this moment on, America's decline is over. (Applause.)

Our liberties and our nation's glorious destiny will no longer be denied. And we will immediately restore the integrity, competency, and loyalty of America's government.

Over the past eight years, I have been tested and challenged more than any president in our 250-year history, and I've learned a lot along the way.

The journey to reclaim our republic has not been an easy one — that, I can tell you. Those who wish to stop our cause have tried to take my freedom and, indeed, to take my life.

Just a few months ago, in a beautiful Pennsylvania field, an assassin's bullet ripped through my ear. But I felt then and believe even more so now that my life was saved for a reason. I was saved by God to make America great again. (Applause.)

Thank you. Thank you. (Applause.)

Thank you very much. (Applause.)

That is why each day under our administration of American patriots, we will be working to meet every crisis with dignity and power and strength. We will move with purpose and speed to bring back hope, prosperity, safety, and peace for citizens of every race, religion, color, and creed.

For American citizens, January 20th, 2025, is Liberation Day. (Applause.) It is my hope that our recent presidential election will be remembered as the greatest and most consequential election in the history of our country.

As our victory showed, the entire nation is rapidly unifying behind our agenda with dramatic increases in support from virtually every element of our society: young and old, men and women, African Americans, Hispanic Americans, Asian Americans, urban, suburban, rural. And very importantly, we had a powerful win in all seven swing states — (applause) — and the popular vote, we won by millions of people. (Applause.)

To the Black and Hispanic communities, I want to thank you for the tremendous outpouring of love and trust that you have shown me with your vote. We set records, and I will not forget it. I've heard your voices in the campaign, and I look forward to working with you in the years to come.

Today is Martin Luther King Day. And his honor — this will be a great honor. But in his honor, we will strive together to make his dream a reality. We will make his dream come true. (Applause.)

Thank you. Thank you. Thank you. (Applause.)

National unity is now returning to America, and confidence and pride is soaring like never before. In everything we do, my administration will be inspired by a strong pursuit of excellence and unrelenting success. We will not forget our country, we will not forget our Constitution, and we will not forget our God. Can't do that. (Applause.)

Today, I will sign a series of historic executive orders. With these actions, we will begin the complete restoration of America and the revolution of common sense. It's all about common sense. (Applause.)

First, I will declare a national emergency at our southern border. (Applause.)

All illegal entry will immediately be halted, and we will begin the process of returning millions and millions of criminal aliens back to the places from which they came. We will reinstate my Remain in Mexico policy. (Applause.)

I will end the practice of catch and release. (Applause.)

And I will send troops to the southern border to repel the disastrous invasion of our country. (Applause.)

Under the orders I sign today, we will also be designating the cartels as foreign terrorist organizations. (Applause.)

And by invoking the Alien Enemies Act of 1798, I will direct our government to use the full and immense power of federal and state law enforcement to eliminate the presence of all foreign gangs and criminal networks bringing devastating crime to U.S. soil, including our cities and inner cities. (Applause.)

As commander in chief, I have no higher responsibility than to defend our country from threats and invasions, and that is exactly what I am going to do. We will do it at a level that nobody has ever seen before.

Next, I will direct all members of my cabinet to marshal the vast powers at their disposal to defeat what was record inflation and rapidly bring down costs and prices. (Applause.)

The inflation crisis was caused by massive overspending and escalating energy prices, and that is why today I will also declare a national energy emergency. We will drill, baby, drill. (Applause.)

America will be a manufacturing nation once again, and we have something that no other manufacturing nation will ever have — the largest amount of oil and gas of any country on earth — and we are going to use it. We'll use it. (Applause.)

We will bring prices down, fill our strategic reserves up again right to the top, and export American energy all over the world. (Applause.)

We will be a rich nation again, and it is that liquid gold under our feet that will help to do it.

With my actions today, we will end the Green New Deal, and we will revoke the electric vehicle mandate, saving our auto industry and keeping my sacred pledge to our great American autoworkers. (Applause.)

In other words, you'll be able to buy the car of your choice.

We will build automobiles in America again at a rate that nobody could have dreamt possible just a few years ago. And thank you to the autoworkers of our nation for your inspiring vote of confidence. We did tremendously with their vote. (Applause.)

I will immediately begin the overhaul of our trade system to protect American workers and families. Instead of taxing our citizens to enrich other countries, we will tariff and tax foreign countries to enrich our citizens. (Applause.)

For this purpose, we are establishing the External Revenue Service to collect all tariffs, duties, and revenues. It will be massive amounts of money pouring into our Treasury, coming from foreign sources. The American dream will soon be back and thriving like never before.

To restore competence and effectiveness to our federal government, my administration will establish the brand-new Department of Government Efficiency. (Applause.)

After years and years of illegal and unconstitutional federal efforts to restrict free expression, I also will sign an executive order to immediately stop all government censorship and bring back free speech to America. (Applause.)

Never again will the immense power of the state be weaponized to persecute political opponents — something I know something about. (Laughter.) We will not allow that to happen. It will not happen again.

Under my leadership, we will restore fair, equal, and impartial justice under the constitutional rule of law. (Applause.)

And we are going to bring law and order back to our cities. (Applause.)

This week, I will also end the government policy of trying to socially engineer race and gender into every aspect of public and private life. (Applause.) We will forge a society that is colorblind and merit-based. (Applause.)

As of today, it will henceforth be the official policy of the United States government that there are only two genders: male and female. (Applause.)

This week, I will reinstate any service members who were unjustly expelled from our military for objecting to the COVID vaccine mandate with full back pay. (Applause.)

And I will sign an order to stop our warriors from being subjected to radical political theories and social experiments while on duty. It's going to end immediately. (Applause.) Our armed forces will be freed to focus on their sole mission: defeating America's enemies. (Applause.)

Like in 2017, we will again build the strongest military the world has ever seen. We will measure our success not only by the battles we win but also by the wars that we end — and perhaps most importantly, the wars we never get into. (Applause.)

My proudest legacy will be that of a peacemaker and unifier. That's what I want to be: a peacemaker and a unifier.

I'm pleased to say that as of yesterday, one day before I assumed office, the hostages in the Middle East are coming back home to their families. (Applause.)

Thank you.

America will reclaim its rightful place as the greatest, most powerful, most respected nation on earth, inspiring the awe and admiration of the entire world.

A short time from now, we are going to be changing the name of the Gulf of Mexico to the Gulf of America — (applause) — and we will restore the name of a great president, William McKinley, to Mount McKinley, where it should be and where it belongs. (Applause.)

President McKinley made our country very rich through tariffs and through talent — he was a natural businessman — and gave Teddy Roosevelt the money for many of the great things he did, including the Panama Canal, which has foolishly been given to the country of Panama after the United Spates — the United States — I mean, think of this — spent more money than ever spent on a project before and lost 38,000 lives in the building of the Panama Canal.

We have been treated very badly from this foolish gift that should have never been made, and Panama's promise to us has been broken.

The purpose of our deal and the spirit of our treaty has been totally violated. American ships are being severely overcharged and not treated fairly in any way, shape, or form. And that includes the United States Navy.

And above all, China is operating the Panama Canal. And we didn't give it to China. We gave it to Panama, and we're taking it back. (Applause.)

Above all, my message to Americans today is that it is time for us to once again act with courage, vigor, and the vitality of history's greatest civilization.

So, as we liberate our nation, we will lead it to new heights of victory and success. We will not be deterred. Together, we will end the chronic disease epidemic and keep our children safe, healthy, and disease-free.

The United States will once again consider itself a growing nation — one that increases our wealth, expands our territory, builds our cities, raises our expectations, and carries our flag into new and beautiful horizons.

And we will pursue our manifest destiny into the stars, launching American astronauts to plant the Stars and Stripes on the planet Mars. (Applause.)

Ambition is the lifeblood of a great nation, and, right now, our nation is more ambitious than any other. There's no nation like our nation.

Americans are explorers, builders, innovators, entrepreneurs, and pioneers. The spirit of the frontier is written into our hearts. The call of the next great adventure resounds from within our souls.

Our American ancestors turned a small group of colonies on the edge of a vast continent into a mighty republic of the most extraordinary citizens on Earth. No one comes close.

Americans pushed thousands of miles through a rugged land of untamed wilderness. They crossed deserts, scaled mountains, braved untold dangers, won the Wild West, ended slavery, rescued millions from tyranny, lifted billions from poverty, harnessed electricity, split the atom, launched mankind into the heavens, and put the universe of human knowledge into the palm of the human hand. If we work together, there is nothing we cannot do and no dream we cannot achieve.

Many people thought it was impossible for me to

stage such a historic political comeback. But as you see today, here I am. The American people have spoken. (Applause.)

I stand before you now as proof that you should never believe that something is impossible to do. In America, the impossible is what we do best. (Applause.)

From New York to Los Angeles, from Philadelphia to Phoenix, from Chicago to Miami, from Houston to right here in Washington, D.C., our country was forged and built by the generations of patriots who gave everything they had for our rights and for our freedom.

They were farmers and soldiers, cowboys and factory workers, steelworkers and coal miners, police officers and pioneers who pushed onward, marched forward, and let no obstacle defeat their spirit or their pride.

Together, they laid down the railroads, raised up the skyscrapers, built great highways, won two world wars, defeated fascism and communism, and triumphed over every single challenge that they faced.

After all we have been through together, we stand on the verge of the four greatest years in American history. With your help, we will restore America promise and we will rebuild the nation that we love — and we love it so much.

We are one people, one family, and one glorious

nation under God. So, to every parent who dreams for their child and every child who dreams for their future, I am with you, I will fight for you, and I will win for you. We're going to win like never before. (Applause.)

Thank you. Thank you. (Applause.)

Thank you. Thank you. (Applause.)

In recent years, our nation has suffered greatly. But we are going to bring it back and make it great again, greater than ever before.

We will be a nation like no other, full of compassion, courage, and exceptionalism. Our power will stop all wars and bring a new spirit of unity to a world that has been angry, violent, and totally unpredictable.

America will be respected again and admired again, including by people of religion, faith, and goodwill. We will be prosperous, we will be proud, we will be strong, and we will win like never before.

We will not be conquered, we will not be intimidated, we will not be broken, and we will not fail.

From this day on, the United States of America will be a free, sovereign, and independent nation.

We will stand bravely, we will live proudly, we will dream boldly, and nothing will stand in our way because we are Americans. The future is ours, and our golden age has just begun.

Thank you. God bless America. Thank you all.

Thank you. (Applause.) Thank you very much. Thank you very much. Thank you. (Applause.) Thank you. (Applause.)

## Remarks by President Trump and Vice President Vance at Liberty Ball

### January 20, 2025 11:27 P.M. EST

Walter E. Washington Convention Center Washington, D.C.

THE VICE PRESIDENT: Good evening, everybody. How are we doing? (Applause.) Are we ready to make America great again? (Applause.)

I just want to say we're so grateful to all of you, so grateful for making sure that we made this election too big to rig, because that's exactly what we did — (applause) and we did it together.

And, of course, I want to thank my dear friend, and I think the best president that this country has had, a man — (applause) — a man who has put everything on the line for the United States of America and gets an opportunity to serve this great country once again: President Donald J. Trump. (Applause.)

So, do we want to hear from the 45th and 47th president of the United States? (Applause.)

Take it away, sir.

THE PRESIDENT: Thank you, JD.

This is a hell of a day we're having, right? (Applause.)

It began very early, and then we decided — you know, we made a good decision, by the way, doing it in the rotunda, as opposed to in about four degrees with the windchill factor. That would not have been pretty.

And, you know, if I made us — did you ever speak in really cold weather? You can't. They would say — the fake news over there, they'd say, "He's cognitively impaired. There's something wrong with him." (Laughter.) So, we didn't want to give them the chance to do that, did we?

We had a — a great time. We had 72-degree temperature in the rotunda. We had the people that we needed. And we had the people that we need tonight, because you guys are unbelievable. We love you all. (Applause.)

And we said a lot of things today. I think we got tremendous reviews on the speech. And, you know, I wanted to put in some really rough stuff, and all of my people, including JD, they said, "You know, let's not put that paragraph in." Oh, I loved that paragraph. (Laughter.) There was a paragraph on "Biden shouldn't be pardoning his family." (Applause.) And we had a couple of others that were far worse than that.

But they said, "You know, the speech is so nice and

it's so unifying." I said, "All right, we won't do it. I'll do it about two hours later." So, we've done — (laughter) — we've been doing it all night long.

But, you know, we're going to turn this country around and fast. (Applause.) We have — we have assets like nobody else. Number one, we have our people. That's our greatest asset, the people of our country. (Applause.)

And I just — and I have a great family. I really do. I — I just look around. My son Eric has been so incredible, married to a woman who became the head of the Republican Party. I wonder, how the hell did that happen? (Applause.) And she's — she really — her and Michael Whatley, from North Carolina, did a great job. (Applause.)

And then you have — where is my Ivanka? Have you ever heard of Ivanka and Jared? (Applause.)

And we have — Tiffany is here someplace. There's Tiffany. Have — with — with child, I have to say. (Applause.) And Michael. Thank you very much.

And what — look at that group back there. That's Kai, our great golfer. She — a great golfer, that one. (Applause.)

And Don and Don and Chloe. Chloe — I don't know, Ivanka, she might be as good as this one. You have to see her athletic ability. You wouldn't believe it. You look at her, she looks so innocent. She's a killer. (Laughter.) Chloe is a killer.

And we have a great vice president, I want to tell you, and a fantastic — (applause) — and he's got a fantastic wife and helper, and she's done — she's done just incredible things for the party and for him. And I want to thank you. Great job. Great job. JD Vance, great job. (Applause.)

So — so, we're going to keep it going. We're going to have it turned around quickly. This big ship, we got to turn it a little bit slower than I'd like, but we're going to turn it around.

We have things that nobody else has. You know, we — we also have something that — it's not politically correct to say, but it's becoming very politically correct: We have more liquid gold under our feet than any other nation in the world. (Applause.) And if you don't mind, we're going to use it, right? (Applause.)

And we just left the Commander in Chief Ball, which is, like, a similar size. Everyone — and we're going to another one in a little while. We needed three because we have such support. There's a longing for competence in this country. There's a longing for common sense in this country.

And I was saying before, with a party of common sense, you know, we — we don't want to have men playing in women's sports. (Applause.) We don't want to have transgender operations for everyone. (Applause.) And we just want to have a great country.

Wan- — we want education. We want houses that don't cost a fortune. We want low interest rates. We want low taxes. We want a strong, powerful military, and we're going to have that.

We did it once. We did it in 2017. We rebuilt our entire military. It was given away, a lot of it. Can you believe it? Given away — so foolishly given away, but we'll have it back again very, very soon.

And we'll be making some announcements. You're going to be so thrilled.

But we love you all. We're going to be — you know, I'd like to say we are a great nation. We will soon be the greatest we've ever been, and that won't take long.

So, I want to thank you all for being here tonight, special people, and we'll see you soon. Just watch what happens. Going to be big progress. (Applause.)

Thank you, everybody. Thank you very much. Thank you. (Applause.)

(The Village People perform "Y.M.C.A.")

MR. WILLIS: Well, all right. President Trump, Vice President Vance. Thank you, sir.

THE PRESIDENT: Ladies and gentlemen, I just want to tell you, they've done something that's never been done before. So, it was, like, about 30 years ago — and I'm trying to be nice — (laughter) — and they did well, but I'm not sure they hit number one. But you know what? They hit number one for the last three weeks, and they are beating every other record — recording. (Applause.) They're the number one show in town, and I want to just congratulate you.

You've been with this song a long time, right?

MR. WILLIS: Yes. I wrote the lyrics to it (inaudible).

THE PRESIDENT: You did?

MR. WILLIS: Yes, sir.

THE PRESIDENT: Well, you're a talented guy.

MR. WILLIS: Thank you, sir.

THE PRESIDENT: Number one, we love it. And you're number one too. Thank you, everybody. And our country is number one, most importantly. (Applause.) Thank you very much.

Congratulations.

MR. WILLIS: Thank you.

THE PRESIDENT: It's a fantastic job.

Thank you. (Applause.)

END 11:38 P.M. EST

## Remarks by President Trump and Vice President Vance at Starlight Ball

### January 21, 2025 12:17 A.M. EST

Union Station Washington, D.C.

THE VICE PRESIDENT: How we doing? (Applause.) Isn't it a great day to make the 45th president of the United States the 47th president of the United States? (Applause.)

Just say, first of all, thank you to all of you for your support, for your kindness, for your friendship, for believing enough in this country to fight for it and make Donald J. Trump the president America needs at this moment in time. (Applause.)

We love you, and we're grateful to you.

And, second, I want to thank the president for his trust that he's placed in me but, most importantly, for the willingness to sacrifice, to serve, to fight through all — let's be honest and call it what it is — fight through all of the lies and the bullshit to serve the American people. (Applause.)

So, I want to introduce the 45th and 47th president of the United States. And we are lucky to have him.

God bless you all. (Applause.)

THE PRESIDENT: Well, thank you very much, JD. And it's great to have you all. And, by the way, JD is doing a great job. You know that. We picked — we picked the right person. (Applause.)

But I especially want to thank the people in this room. You know, many of you are donors. Some of you are large donors. You believed in us very early. Some of you believed in us from 2015. (Applause.) But you believed in us — there's a lot of people out there.

And — and 2016 was a great year. And then we did much better in 2020, much — we got 10 or 12 million more votes. And I don't know what happened, but I knew — I said, "We're doing this again. We're going to make it too big to rig." And that's what happened.

We had the best numbers anyone has ever seen in the history of the Republican Party, actually. Got the biggest vote in the history of the Republican Party and I guess in most of the history of the Democrat Party too, because we won in a landslide. We won the seven swing states, and we won the popular vote. It's nice to be popular. It's very nice to be popular. (Applause.) And we won it — we won it by millions of votes.

So, I just want to thank everybody, because this really is a very special room. And this is the one we chose to come to last. That's supposed to be a good thing, and it is a good thing, because we have so many friends in the crowd but, really, friends that supported us.

We had a — an incredible day today at the inauguration, and I've gotten good reviews on the speech. You know, they made me take some of the rather difficult things — Melania said to me, "You know, you could do without a couple of those paragraphs."

(Laughter.) And we listened, and we listened to some others.

We have some tremendous professionals. Susie Wiles is doing a fantastic job. (Applause.) (Inaudible.)

And we had great people — great people on the campaign. The campaign was so beautiful. That last 120 days, I didn't sleep one night. I mean, literally, we just kept going, going, going — no days off, no vacation days. And we kept hearing the other side was going to take a couple of days off during the week.

I remember there were 14 days, then 17 days, and I heard that our opponent was going to take about 5 days off. I said, "How do you do that when you're going for the big one?" (Laughter.)

But we worked very hard. And I really think we outworked them, but we also out-thought them. Work is wonderful, but you have to be able to think.

And now we have the job of bringing our country back because we have the embarrassment of having other countries dumping prisoners and mental institution patients into our country with a stupid open border.

As you know, the border was closed at exactly 1:05 in the afternoon today. (Applause.) And I don't mean closed; I mean really closed. It's closed.

And we're going to — we have no choice. It's not that I want to do this. Dwight Eisenhower, a very moderate president, has the record. He just couldn't stand when people poured into the country. He has the record for getting people out that shouldn't be here. And, you know, we're going to far exceed that — not that I want to brag about it, because I hate having to do it.

They should have never done this to our country. They should have never let this happen. You know that this is happening with countries all over the world, and you know their crime rates are going down by 10 and 15 and 20 percent every six months? Venezuela, their crime rate is down by 74.2 percent because they took their street criminals, their prisoners, and their mental patients, and they brought them into the United States of America. Who the hell can think that's a good thing? But we're getting them out, and we're strengthening everything we have.

We have something that nobody else has. We have more liquid gold under our feet than any other country in the world. (Applause.) And if you don't mind — now, if you do mind, I will not do it — if you don't mind, we're going to use it. We're going to use it.

And — and through a system of good deals and renegotiating all of these terrible deals — we made some good — really good ones in 2016, but some of the best ones we made were terminated by this

Biden administration and gave them back everything they wanted, these other countries, even if they're allies.

And we have some allies from countries right in this room — big, big people in countries. So, I hate to embarrass them, but some of our allies are really — they treat us worse than the enemies on trade. We're not going to let that happen.

So, we're going to do things that really started three months ago. We won the election, and that was a big, big — November 5th, that was a big day. And I want to make that the most consequential election in the history of our country. It's going to be the most consequential.

We're going to turn it around very fast. It's a big, big ship, but we're turning it as fast as a big ship can be turned. And we're going to make America great again. (Applause.)

And I just want to thank everybody in — in this large room, because it's packed. And the beautiful thing is we have two other rooms that are massive, and you couldn't get in. No matter what you did, you couldn't get in. And it's just a great tribute to everybody here and to the people on stage.

My family has been so great. Everyone in this — on this floor.

Did — has anybody ever heard of Eric Trump? (Applause.) He's got more subpoenas than anybody in the history of the United States. (Laughter.) They were after their political opponent. How did that work out? Not so good.

They got us a lot of votes. Can you believe it? That's the first time that's ever happened, actually.

But I just want to thank everybody very much, and I want to thank our first lady. People love our first lady. (Applause.) And she's done a fantastic job.

And we're going to have a tremendous four years, and hopefully it's going to go long beyond four years. We have some tremendous talent, including this guy right here. Hopefully, it's going to go long beyond four years.

So, again, I want to thank you for your confidence. I want to especially thank those people — JD — that were here in 2015 before I really started. And there's a lot of them in the room, and they just stuck. And they said, "We got to do it again, sir. We got to do it again." And we did it again, and we won in record fashion. So, it was a landslide. It was a mandate like nobody has had before.

So, thank you all very much. We love you all. And we're going to do a real job for you. Thank you. Thank you very much, everybody. (Applause.)

# Remarks by President Trump at the World Economic Forum via Teleconference

## January 23, 2025 11:06 A.M. EST

THE PRESIDENT: Well, thank you very much, Klaus. And hello to everyone in beautiful Davos. This has been a truly historic week in the United States. Three days ago, I took the oath of office, and we began the golden age of America. The recent presidential election was won by millions of votes and all seven — every one of them — all seven swing states. It was a massive mandate from the American people like hasn't been seen in many years. And some of the political pundits, even some of my so-called enemies, said it was the most consequential election victory in 129 years. That's quite nice.

What the world has witnessed in the past 72 hours is nothing less than a revolution of common sense. Our country will soon be stronger, wealthier, and more united than ever before, and the entire planet will be more peaceful and prosperous as a result of this incredible momentum and what we're doing and going to do.

My administration is acting with unprecedented speed to fix the disasters we've inherited from a totally inept group of people and to solve every single crisis facing our country.

This begins with confronting the economic chaos caused by the failed policies of the last administration. Over the past four years, our government racked up $8 trillion in wasteful deficit spending and inflicted nation-wrecking energy restrictions, crippling regulations, and hidden taxes like never before. The result is the worst inflation crisis in modern history and sky-high interest rates for our citizens and even throughout the world. Food prices and the price of almost every other thing known to mankind went through the roof.

President Biden totally lost control of what was going on in our country but, in particular, with our high-inflation economy and at our border. Because of these ruinous policies, total government spending this year is $1.5 trillion higher than was projected to occur when I left office just four years ago. Likewise, the cost of servicing the debt is more than 230 percent higher than was projected in 2020.

The inflation rate we are inheriting remains 50 percent higher than the historic target. It was the highest inflation probably in the history of our country. That's why, from the moment I took office, I've taken rapid action to reverse each and every one of these radical left policies that created this calamity — in particular, with immigration, crime, and inflation.

On day one, I signed an executive order directing every member of my Cabinet to marshal all powers at their disposal to defeat inflation and reduce the cost of daily life. I imposed a federal hiring freeze, a federal regulation freeze, a foreign aid freeze, and I created the new Department of Government Efficiency.

I terminated the ridiculous and incredibly wasteful Green New Deal — I call it the "Green New Scam"; withdrew from the one-sided Paris Climate Accord; and ended the insane and costly electric vehicle mandate. We're going to let people buy the car they want to buy.

I declared a national em- — energy emergency — and it's so important — national energy emergency to unlock the liquid gold under our feet and pave the way for rapid approvals of new energy infrastructure. The United States has the largest amount of oil and gas of any country on Earth, and we're going to use it.

Not only will this reduce the cost of virtually all goods and services, it will make the United States a manufacturing superpower and the world capital of artificial intelligence and crypto.

My administration has also begun the largest deregulation campaign in history, far exceeding even the record-setting efforts of my last term.

In total, the Biden administration imposed $50,000

in additional regulatory costs on the average American household over the last four years. I have promised to eliminate 10 old regulations for every new regulation, which will soon put many thousands of dollars back in the pockets of American families.

To further unleash our economy, our majorities in the House and Senate — which we also took, along with the presidency — are going to pass the largest tax cut in American history, including massive tax cuts for workers and family and big tax cuts for domestic producers and manufacturers. And we're working with the Democrats on getting an extension of the original Trump tax cuts, as you probably know by just reading any paper.

My message to every business in the world is very simple: Come make your product in America, and we will give you among the lowest taxes of any nation on Earth. We're bringing them down very substantially, even from the original Trump tax cuts. But if you don't make your product in America, which is your prerogative, then, very simply, you will have to pay a tariff — differing amounts, but a tariff — which will direct hundreds of billions of dollars and even trillions of dollars into our Treasury to strengthen our economy and pay down debt.

Under the Trump administration, there will be no better place on Earth to create jobs, build factories, or grow a company than right here in the good old

USA.

Already, American's economic — and you can see this, I think, maybe even in your — in your wonderful, wonderful room that you're all gathered together — so many of my friends — but, Americans, the economic confidence is soaring like we haven't seen in many, many decades, maybe not at all.

Upon my election, it was just announced that small-business optimism skyrocketed by 41 points in a single month. That's the highest ever. There's never been anything like that.

SoftBank has announced between a $100 and $200 billion investment in the U.S. economy because of the election result. And just two days ago, Oracle, SoftBank, and OpenAI announced a $500 billion investment in AI infrastructure. Other companies, likewise, have announced billions and billions and billions — adding up to trillions — of investment in America, in the United States.

And it's also reported today in the papers that Saudi Arabia will be investing at least $600 billion in America. But I'll be asking the crown prince, who's a fantastic guy, to round it out to around $1 trillion. I think they'll do that because we've been very good to them. And I'm also going to ask Saudi Arabia and OPEC to bring down the cost of oil. You got to bring it down, which, frankly, I'm surprised they didn't do before the election. That didn't show a lot of love by them not doing it. I was a little surprised by that.

If the price came down, the Russia-Ukraine war would end immediately. Right now, the price is high enough that that war will continue. You got to bring down the oil price; you're going to end that war. They should have done it long ago. They're very responsible, actually, to a certain extent, for what's taking place — millions of lives are being lost.

With oil prices going down, I'll demand that interest rates drop immediately. And, likewise, they should be dropping all over the world. Interest rates should follow us.

All over, the progress that you're seeing is happening because of our historic victory in a recent presidential election, one that has become quite well known throughout the world.

I think a lot of things are happening to a lot of countries. They say that there's light shining all over the world since the election. And even countries that we aren't particularly friendly with are happy because they understand what — there is a future and th- — how great the future will be.

Under our leadership, America is back and open for business. And this week, I'm also taking swift action to stop the invasion at our southern border. They allowed people to come in at levels that nobody has ever seen before. It was ridiculous. I decided a — and declared to dec- — to — to do — and very, very importantly — a national emergency on our border; immediately halted all entry of illegal border crossers, of which there were many; and began properly returning the illegal trespassers back to the place from which they came.

That action, as you've probably seen, has already started very strongly. I have deployed active-duty U.S. military and National Guard troops to the border to assist in repelling the invasion. It was really an invasion. We will not allow our territory to be violated.

After four long years, the United States is strong and sovereign and a beautiful nation once again. It's a strong, sovereign nation.

In addition, I'm pleased to report that America is also a free nation once again. On day one, I signed an executive order to stop all government censorship. No longer will our government label the speech of our own citizens as misinformation or disinformation, which are the favorite words of censors and those who wish to stop the free exchange of ideas and, frankly, progress. We have saved free speech in America, and we've saved it strongly.

With another historic executive order this week, I also ended the weaponization of law enforcement against the American people — and, frankly, against politicians — and restored the fair, equal, and impartial rule of law.

My administration has taken action to abolish all discriminatory diversity, equity, and inclusion nonsense — and these are policies that were absolute nonsense — throughout the government and the private sector. With the recent, yet somewhat unexpected, great Supreme Court decision just made, America will once again become a merit-based country. You have to hear that word: merit-based country.

And I've made it official — an official policy of the United States that there are only two genders, male and female, and we will have no men participating in women's sports, and transgender operations, which became the rage, will occur very rarely.

Finally, as we restore common sense in America, we're moving quickly to bring back strength and peace and stability abroad. I'm also going to ask all NATO nations to increase defense spending to 5 percent of GDP, which is what it should have been years ago — it was only at 2 percent, and most nations didn't pay until I came along; I insisted that they pay, and they did — because the United States was really paying the difference at that time, and it's — it was unfair to the United States. But many, many things have been unfair for many years to the

United States.

Before even taking office, my team negotiated a cease-fire agreement in the Middle East, which wouldn't have happened without us, as I think most of the people in the room know. Earlier this week, the hostages began to return to their families. They are returning, and it's a beautiful sight. And they'll be coming in more and more. They started coming back on Sunday.

Our efforts to secure a peace settlement between Russia and Ukraine are now, hopefully, underway. It's so important to get that done. That is an absolute killing field.

Millions of soldiers are being killed. Nobody has seen anything like it since World War II. They're laying dead all over the flat fields. It's a flat field — farmland, and there's millions of Russians and millions of Ukrainians. Nobody's seen anything like it since World War II. It's time to end it.

And here in America, we have big events coming up. Next year we have the 250th anniversary of America's founding. I'm so honored to be president during that. That's been a big event. They've been talking about it for 10 years. We also have the World Cup, and I understand Gianni — Gianni is in the room — Infantino. He was very instrumental in helping us get it — he's there with you someplace, I think — and I want to thank him for that.

And then we have the Olympics coming up, which I was instrumental in getting, also, in my first term. And who would have known that by skipping a term, I would get the Olympics? I was upset. I said, "You know, I got the Olympics to come and I won't be president." But it turned out, through a stroke of luck or whatever you might call it, that I'm going to be president during the World Cup and the Olympics and the 250th

anniversary. So, that's going to be three big events.

And we've accomplished more in less than four days — we have really been working — four days — than other administrations have accomplished in four years, and we're just getting started. It's really an amazing thing to see, and the spirit and the light over our country has been incredible.

Under the last administration, our nation has suffered greatly, but we are going to bring it back and make it greater, bigger, stronger, better than ever before.

I want to thank everybody for being with you. I would have been there myself, except the inauguration was two days ago. I thought it might be a little bit quick to make it the first stop, but we'll get there one day. We hope to get there.

But I — I do appreciate — I heard the audience is fantastic, and many of my friends are in the audience. And I will be taking questions now from some very distinguished people.

Thank you all very much. (Applause.)

MR. BRENDE: Thank you. Thank you very much, Mr. President, for that very powerful speech, and I think you could hear the applause all the way from Davos to the White House. But next year, it will be even better, because then you can get the applause here in Davos. So, we wish you welcome to our village next year. We hope to see you.

THE PRESIDENT: Thank you very much.

MR. BRENDE: So, we also know, Mr. President, that you open up for interaction here. We have a great panel with some of the most distinguished businesspeople in the world.

Let me start with someone that you know really well, that I think is almost a neighbor of you in Mal-a- — in — in Florida, Mr. Steve Schwarzman, chairman, CEO, and cofounder of Blackstone Group. So, Steve, floor is yours.

MR. SCHWARZMAN: Well, Mr. President —

THE PRESIDENT: Hello, Steve.

MR. SCHWARZMAN: — I'm sure the crown prince of Saudi Arabia will be really glad you gave this speech today. (Laughter.)

THE PRESIDENT: I hope so.

MR. SCHWARZMAN: You've had the busiest four days that anybody can imagine, and congratulations for that.

And my question is — is about some of the things I've observed here at Davos. It's a terrific forum. I've met lots of people, as usual. I think I've been here 30 years. And a lot of the European businesspeople have expressed enormous frustration with the regulatory regime in the EU, and they attribute slower growth rates here because of numerous factors, but especially because of regulations.

And you've taken a completely different approach in this area. And if you could explain the theory of what you're doing, how you're going to do it, and what you expect the outcome to be, I'd appreciate it.

THE PRESIDENT: Well, thank you very much. And congratulations, Steve — you're a friend of mine — but on a great career. You have had an amazing career and continues. So, I just want to congratulate you. Very inspirational to a lot of people.

I want to talk about the EU, because you mentioned specifically that I've also had a lot of friends and leaders of countries. I've gotten to know them all my first term and a little bit during this period of four years and know them well, like them a lot, but they're very frustrated because of the time everything seems to take to get approved — environmental impact statements for things that you shouldn't even have to do that, and many, many other ways that it takes.

And I'm going to give you a quick little example. I w- — in the private life, my beautiful private life — before I had all these things happening — the world is a little different — I had a nice, simple life. You knew that.

But when I had that simple life, I did projects, and I had a big project in Ireland, and it had to get approval on something that would have made it even better. And I got the approval from Ireland in a period of a week, and it was a very, very, very efficient, good approval.

And they informed me, though, "The problem is you're going to have to get it from the EU, and we think that'll take five to six years." And I said, "You have to be kidding." And this was before politics. And I said, "Wait a minute. It's not that important. I don't want to go five or six years." But it would have been a big investment. It would have been nice, and it would have been good for the project.

And I sent the people to the EU to see if they could speed it up, and basically it was a five- or six-year wait just to get a simple approval that Ireland gave me in a period of, literally, not much more than a week.

And I realized right then — that was the first time I

really was involved with the EU, but I realized right then, that's a problem, and I didn't even bother applying to do it, and — or if I did, I pulled it very quickly. I don't wa- — I have to be very accurate, because I don't want to be criticized. "He did apply, actually." No, I want to be very accurate. So, I don't think I did, but if I did, I pulled it very quickly. It was just something you — you couldn't wait five years or six years to get an approval.

So, a lot of — in a very big business sense, a lot of people are — are claiming that's the problem.

From the standpoint of America, the EU treats us very, very unfairly, very badly. They have a large tax that we know about and — a VAT tax — and it's a very substantial one. They don't take our far- — essentially, don't take our farm products and they don't take our cars. Yet, they send cars to us by the millions.

They put tariffs on things that we want to do, like, for instance, I think they actually — in terms of these are noneconomic or nonmonetary tariffs, and — and those are very bad, and they make it very difficult to bring products into Europe, and yet they expect to be selling and they do sell their products in the United States.

So, we have, you know, hundreds of billions of dollars of deficits with the EU, and nobody is happy with it. And we're going to do something about it, but nobody is happy with it. So, I think the EU has to speed up their process.

Friends of mine that are in some of the nations within the EU, great people, they — they want to be able to compete better, and you can't compete when you can't get — go through the approval process fast. There's no reason why it can't go faster.

So, you know, I'm — I'm trying to be constructive, because I love Europe. I love the countries of Europe. But the process is a very cumbersome one, and th- — and they do treat the United States of America very, very unfairly with the VAT taxes and all of the other taxes they impose.

One other — just to finish up, I got a call from the head of a major airline, one of the biggest airlines in the world. And he said, "Sir, could you help us?" "What?" "Landing in Europe is brutal. They charge us fees for everything, and it's so unfair." I said, "How does it compare to China?" He said, "It's — it's much worse."

And the other thing, as you know, they took court cases with Apple, and they supposedly won a case that most people didn't think was much of a case. They won $15 or $16 billion from Apple. They won billions from Google. I think they're after Facebook for billions and billions.

These are American companies. Whether you like them or not, they're — they're American companies, and they shouldn't be doing that. And that's — as far as I'm concerned, it's a form of taxation.

So, we have some very big complaints with the EU.

Thank you.

MR. BRENDE: Tha- — thank you very much, Mr. President. We'll now go to one of your friends in the EU, Patrick Pouyanné. He's the chairman and CEO of TotalEnergies.

I guess you have a question ready, Patrick, for the president.

MR. POUYANNÉ: Mr. President, as we understand, energy is at the top of your agenda, and it's an honor for me to represent the energy industry tonight in this panel. TotalEnergies is indeed the fourth largest oil and gas and electricity company in the world.

I will not ask you a question about the oil price. It's quite clear what you expect from us. I will more go to gas more. And we, our company, is the largest, number one exporter LNG from the U.S. company. We are a strong contributor to and we invest in mammoth LNG projects in Texas, $20 billion. It's far from $200, but it's $20 billion. And we contribute with that to security of supply to Europe as we export this LNG to Europe.

Some experts fear that if there are too many projects developed in the U.S. on LNG, this could have an inflat- — inflationary impact on the U.S. domestic gas price, and they recommend a pause on these projects.

I would ask you the following question: What are your views on — about such a pause on investments on LNG in the U.S.? What would happen if you would observe an increased domestic gas price because of these exports? And final question, which is important for Europe: Would you agree to guarantee security of supplies of U.S. LNG to Europe?

THE PRESIDENT: Well, on the last part of your question, yes, I would. I would make sure that you get it. If we make a deal, we make a deal; you'll get it. Because a lot of people do have that problem. They make a deal, and then it can't get supplied because of war-type problems and other problems. So, we would absolutely do that.

LNG is very interesting, because when I took office for the first term, one of the first things I looked at was two — there were two very massive plants in Louisiana, a state that has been very good to me. I won it by many, many points, and

I felt strongly indebted to it, actually.

And they said there are two plants that have been under environmental consideration for more than 10 years, and they were costing — as you say, you know how expensive those plants are — but they were costing like $12 billion and, I think, $14 or $15 billion. But they couldn't get their permits. It was — they were in review for years — many, many years — like a decade or more.

And I said, "So ridiculous." I know so much about that, because in the construction industry, I had to go through it too, but I got good at it after a while.

But I — I went — I saw the projects, and you're talking about a total investment of $25 to $30 billion, and it looked like it was going to end. They couldn't get their permits, and I got them done in less than a week. It was done, completed.

In fact, when they called them to announce that it was done, the countries — largely countries — Japan was involved and — and another country and some very big investors — they couldn't believe it. They actually couldn't believe it.

And I said, "Just do yourself one favor. Don't pay any consultants, because the only one that got it done was me." I got it done because it was the right thing to do for the U.S. and for the world, but the consultants had nothing to do with it, you know? The consultants go in and they say, "Give us millions of dollars because Trump did it." Nobody called me about it. I just heard it was a problem for years, and I got it done because it was the right thing to do for the U.S. and the right thing to do for beyond. It had to do with energy — very important.

So, I think it's very important. I think the — the

— you know, I disagree with one. I think the more that you do, the lower the price is going to go. And what I'd like to see is rapid approvals.

We're going to give very rapid approvals in the United States, like with the AI plants, talking to — many people want to build them. That's going to be a very big thing.

We're going to build electric generating facilities — they are going to build. I'm going to get them the approval. Under emergency declaration, I can get the approvals done myself without having to go through years of waiting.

And the big problem is we need double the energy we currently have in the United States — can you imagine? — for AI to really be as big as we want to have it. Because it's a very competitive — it will be very competitive with China and others.

So, I'm going to give emergency declarations so that they can start building them almost immediately.

And I'm — I'm — I think it was largely my idea, because nobody thought this was possible. It wasn't that they were not smart, because they're the smartest, but I told them that what I want you to do is build your electric generating plant right next to your plant as a separate building, connected. And they said, "Wow, you're kidding." And I said, "No, no. I'm not kidding." You don't have to hook into the grid, which is old and, you know, could be taken out. If it's taken out, they wouldn't have any way to get any electricity.

So, we are going to allow them to go on a very rapid bas- — basis to build their plant — build the electric generating plant. They can fuel it with anything they want, and they may have coal as a backup. Good, clean coal.

You know, if there were a problem with a — with a pipe coming in — as an example, you're going with gas — oil or gas — and a pipe gets blown up or, for some reason, doesn't work, there are some companies in the U.S. that have coal sitting right by the plant so that if there's an emergency, they can go to that short-term basis and use our very clean coal.

So, that's something else that a lot of people didn't even know about. But nothing can destroy coal — not the weather, not a bomb — nothing. It might make it a little smaller, might make it a little different shape. But coal is very strong as a backup. It's a great backup to have that facility, and it wouldn't cost much more — more money.

And we have more coal than anybody. We also have more oil and gas than anybody.

So, we're going to make it so that the plants will have their own electric generating facilities attached right to their plant. They don't have to worry about a utility. They don't have to worry about anything. And we're going to get very rapid approvals.

MR. BRENDE: Thank you. Thank you so much, Mr. President. We'll now go to another CEO that you know very well: Brian Moynihan, the CEO and chair of Bank of America.

MR. MOYNIHAN: Good afternoon, Mr. President, and congratulations — an obviously eventful week for you and your family.

If you remember, five years ago, you came here and we walked among 150 CEOs from all over the world, and you engaged with them about your policies and your procedures.

This year, you're not here. And yet this week was eventful, from the orders that you mentioned earlier — literally a wave of orders coming out on immigration, on trade, and many other matters.

And so, as a representative of the United States here, we got a lot of questions about what does all this mean and how would the president square this with his clear focus on growth, prosperity, market gro- — stock market growth, a good bond market, and bringing down prices.

So, how do you think about the impact of all these orders and how fast they come out and how you're going to balance them with that scorecard of being successful on both contan- — continuing GDP growth, bringing down inflation, and also having a good stock price appreciation for the American citizen?

THE PRESIDENT: Well, I think it's going to actually bring down inflation. It's going to bring up jobs. We're going to have a lot of jobs. We're going to have a lot of companies moving in.

You know, Brian, we're at 21 percent. It was at 40 percent, and I got it down to 21 percent — the corporate tax. And it was — actually, if you look at state and city, it was, in many cases, much higher than 40 percent. I got it down to 21 percent. And now we're going to bring it down from 21 to 15 percent if — this is a big "if" — if you make your product in the U.S.

So, we're going to have the lowest — just about the lowest rate. It will be — the 21 is on the low side worldwide; the 15 is about as low as it gets, and by far the lowest of a large country — a large, you know, rich, powerful country — by far, not even a contest.

So, we're going to bring it down to 15 percent if you make your product in the USA. So, that's going to create a — a tremendous buzz.

We're also probably going back to the one-year deduction, where we deduct — you know, we — we did that originally, and that was amazing what — the impact that that had, the one-year deduction, which built up over a period of time and then it expires. But we're going to go back to that when we do the renewal of the Trump tax plan.

We have to get Democrats to approve it. But, you

know, if the Democrats didn't approve it, I don't know how they can survive with about a 45 percent tax increase, because that's what it would be. And so, I think they're going to b- — w- — we've been working along with them pretty well.

I think it's very hard for a political group to say, "Let's charge people 45 percent more." So, I think we're in good shape.

But we're actually doing a reduction for business and small businesses, where you're going to b- — bring it down to 15 percent, which is really something.

And, by the way, speaking of you — and you've done a fantastic job — but I hope you start opening your bank to conservatives, because many conservatives complain that the banks are not allowing them to do business within the bank, and that included a place called Bank of America. They conserv- — they don't take conservative business. And I don't know if the regulators mandated that because of Biden or what, but you and Jamie and everybody, I hope you're going to open your banks to conservatives, because what you're doing is wrong.

MR. MOYNIHAN: Mr. President —

MR. BRENDE: (Inaudible.)

MR. MOYNIHAN: — I'll say that your friend Gianni was — said hello — told me tell you hello, and we look forward to sponsoring the World Cup when it comes, both this summer for the club and next year. So, thank you for getting that for the United States.

THE PRESIDENT: Thank you very much, Brian.

MR. BRENDE: Thank you, Mr. President. We'll now go to Ana Botín. She's the executive chairman of Banco Santander, one of the big European banks and also in the U.S.

So, Ana.

MS. BOTÍN: Mr. President, congratulations on a historic victory.

THE PRESIDENT: Thank you.

MS. BOTÍN: I believe you don't know me as well as my fellow panelists, so a few words. Santander is one of the largest banks in the world by number of customers, 170 million. That's more than my friend Brian or my friend Jamie have. (Laughter.)

THE PRESIDENT: Wow.

MS. BOTÍN: And those — (applause) —

MR. MOYNIHAN: If they fix the regulation (inaudible).

MS. BOTÍN: That's coming. That's coming.

MR. BRENDE: That was cheeky. (Laughter.)

MS. BOTÍN: We are — we are a big investor in the United States. We have many million customer, 12,000 employees. We're one of the largest auto lenders, and we recently launched a fully digital bank called Openbank.

We strongly believe banks have a pivotal role in the economy, and we can accelerate growth and help many more customers. That's what we do in the United States. So, as Brian pointed out, we very much welcome your focus on deregulation and reducing bureaucracy.

So, my question is: What are your priorities in this regard, and how fast is this going to happen? Thank you very much.

THE PRESIDENT: Well, I think it's going to — thank you and congratulations. I know very much about your bank, and you've done a fantastic job. Congratulations.

We are going to move very quickly. We've moved very quickly. We've done things in the last three days that nobody thought were possible to do in years. And it's all taken — it's all taken effect. It's going to have a huge impact on the economy, a huge positive impact. Money was being wasted on crazy things.

I mean, the Green New Deal was such a total disgrace — what — what — how that was perpetrated. And it was conceived of by people that were average students — less than average students, I might add — and never even took a course in energy or the environment. It was just a game. Remember, the world was going to end in 12 years? Remember that? Well, the 12 years has come and gone.

It was going to end. It was going to all foam into earth. But, you know, the time has come.

The — these people — and they — they really — they really scared the Democrats large- — I can't say the Republicans. Republicans maybe could have fought harder to stop it, but it's been a tremendous waste of — a tremendous waste of money.

You know, during my four years, we had the cleanest air, we had the cleanest water, and yet we had the most productive economy in the history of our country. We had the most productive economy. Until COVID came, we had the most productive in the history of our country, by far.

And — and actually, you could look worldwide, we — we're — we were beating everybody from China to everybody else. So — and we think we really — now, with what we have learned and all of the other things that have taken place, we think we can even far surpass that — a- — actually, far, far surpass it. But we do — one thing we're going to be demanding is we're going to — be demanding respect from other nations.

Canada. We have a tremendous deficit with Canada. We're not going to have that anymore. We can't do it. It's — it's — I don't know if it's good for them. As you probably know, I say, "You can always become a state, and if you're a state, we won't have a deficit. We won't have to tariff you, et cetera, et cetera."

But Canada has been very tough to deal with over the years, and it's not fair that we should have a $200 billion or $250 billion deficit. We don't need them to make our cars, and they make a lot of them. We don't need their lumber because we have our own forests, et cetera, et cetera. We don't need their oil and gas. We have our — we have more than anybody.

So, you know, just as an example, with Mexico — we're dealing with Mexico, I think, very well. And we're just — you know, w- — we just want to be treated fairly with other nations, because there's hardly a nation in the world — and I blame this on us, and I blame it on politicians that for some reason — and probably mostly it's stupidity, but you could also say other reasons, but mostly stupidity — they've allowed other nations to take advantage of the U.S. And w- — we can't allow that to happen anymore.

You know, we have debt. It's a very small debt when you compare it to value — the value of the assets that we have, but we don't want to do that. We want to just have debt be obliterated, and we'll be able to do that fairly rapidly. And a lot of good things are going to happen.

And — and honestly, good things are going to happen for the world, and good things are going to happen for the people that are dealing with us — allies and beyond allies.

One thing — very important — I really would like to be able to meet with President Putin soon and get that war end — ended, and — and that's not from the standpoint of economy or anything else. It's from the standpoint of millions of lives are being wasted. Beautiful, young people are being shot in the battlefield. You know, the bullet — a very flat land, as I said, and the bullet goes — there's no — there's no hiding. And a bullet — the only thing going to stop the bullet is a human body. And you have to see — I've seen pictures of what's taken place. It's a carnage.

And we really have to stop that war. That war is horrible. And I'm not talking economy, I'm not talking economics, I'm not talking about natural resource. I'm just talking about: There's so many young people being killed in this war, and that's not including the people that have been killed as the cities are being, you know, knocked down building by building. So, we really should get that stopped.

Likewise, in the Middle East, I think we've made a lot of progress in the Middle East, and I think that's going to — that's going to come along pretty well.

Thank you very much.

MR. BRENDE: Thank you, Mr. President. We

know that most consequential relationship in the world is between the U.S. and China. U.S., 28 percent of the global economy; China close to 20. That's almost half of the global GDP.

And we know that you called President Xi Jinping last Friday. We heard that you had a good discussion.

How do you see the relationship between the U.S. and China in the next four years under your leadership?

THE PRESIDENT: He called me. But I see it very good. I think that we're going to have a very good relationship. All we want is fairness. We just want a level playing field. We don't want to take advantage. We've been having massive deficits with China. Biden allowed it to get out of hand. He's — $1.1 trillion deficit. It's ridiculous, and it's just an unfair relationship.

And we have to make it just fair. We don't have to make it phenomenal. We have to make it a fair relationship. Right now, it's not a fair relationship. The deficit is massive, as it is with other countries — a lot of Asian countries, actually. But we have deficits that are very big, and we can't keep doing that, so we're not going to keep doing that.

But I like President Xi very much. I've always liked him. We always had a very good relationship. It was very strained with COVID coming out of Wuhan.

Obviously, that strained it. I'm sure it strained it with a lot of people, but that strained our relationship. But we always had a great relationship, I would say, and we look forward to doing very well with China and getting along with China.

Hopefully, China can help us stop the war with, in particular, Russia-Ukraine. And they have a great deal of power over that situation, and we'll work with them.

And I mentioned that with — during our phone conversation with President Xi, and hopefully we could work together and get that stopped.

We'd like to see denuclearization. In fact, with President Putin, prior to a — an election result, which was, frankly, ridiculous, we were talking about denuclearization of our two countries, and China would have come along. China has a — a much smaller, right now, nuclear armament than us or field than us, but they're — they're going to be catching it at some point over the next four or five years.

And I will tell you that President Putin really liked the idea of — of cutting way back on nuclear. And I think the rest of the world, we would have gotten them to follow. And China would have come along too. China also liked it.

Tremendous amounts of money are being spent on nuclear, and the destructive capability is something that we don't even want to talk about today, because you don't want to hear it. It's too depressing.

So, we want to see if we can denuclearize, and I think that's very possible. And I can tell you that President Putin wanted to do it. He and I wanted to do it. We had a good conversation with China. They would have been involved, and that would have been an unbelievable thing for the planet.

And I hope —

MR. BRENDE: Mr. President, when you're —

THE PRESIDENT: — it can be started up again.

MR. BRENDE: — back here in Davos next year, will — will there be then a peace agreement with — with Ukraine and Russia by then?

THE PRESIDENT: Well, you're going to have to ask Russia. Ukraine is ready to — to make a deal. Just so you understand, this is a war that should have never started. If I were president, it would never have started. This is a war that should have never, ever been started. And — and it wasn't started during my — there was never even talk about it. I knew that it was the apple of President Putin's eye, but I also knew that there was no way he was going in, and he wasn't going to go in.

And then, when I was out, bad things happened, bad things were said, a lot of stupidity all around, and you end up with what you have. Now you have all these bombed-out cities — they look like demolition sites — with many people killed.

I think the — the thing that you'll see about Ukraine is that far — far more people have died than is being reported. And I've seen that. But far, far more people have died.

When you look at a city that's become a demolition site, where big buildings have been collapsed by missiles hitting them and everything else, and they say, "One person was slightly injured." No, no, many people were killed. Those are big buildings. I was surprised at how — that was my business. These are buildings that go two and three blocks long. They're 20 stories high. They're big, powerful buildings. Then they were knocked down, and there were a lot of people in those buildings. They had announced that two people were injured. That's not true. So, I think you're going to find that there were many more people killed in Ukraine and the Ukraine war than anybody has any idea.

But if you look now, so many of the — the people being killed are soldiers just facing each other with guns, rifles, and drones — the new form of warfare — drones. And it's a very sad thing to see.

And when you see pictures of the fields that I see, nobody wants to see it. You'll never be the same.

MR. BRENDE: Thank you very much, Mr. President. On behalf of all the 3,000 participants here in Davos, we really, really underline that joining us, the third day in your presidency, live, taking questions here, it's so appreciated. And we are already ready for receiving you next year in person.

So, thank you very much, and all the best from Davos. (Applause.)

THE PRESIDENT: Thank you. Thank you very much. Thank you. (Applause.)

END 11:49 A.M. EST

## Remarks by President Trump at Executive Order Signing

### January 23, 2025 3:10 P.M. EST

Oval Office

THE PRESIDENT: Hello, everybody.

Q Hello, sir.

THE PRESIDENT: You all set? Okay. Very good. I'm going to sign some executive orders. They are very important in just about every case. And we'll go through the first one, please.

MR. SCHARF: Sure. Do you want to —

MR. SACKS: Yeah. Mr. President, this is an executive order on crypto. We're going to be —

MR. SCHARF: That's AI. Sorry.

MR. SACKS: Oh, sorry. We're doing AI first. Sorry.

MR. SCHARF: Yeah, AI.

MR. SACKS: Sir, this is an executive order on AI. We're forming — we're — we're basically announc-

ing the administration's policy to make America the — the world capital in artificial intelligence and to dominate and to lead the world in AI.
THE PRESIDENT: Do you want to say your name — your full name and serial number?
MR. SACKS: Yeah, David Sacks, AI and crypto czar.
THE PRESIDENT: David is one of the greatest in the world at AI — most respected, probably, there is.
(The executive order is signed.)
So, that should take us to the forefront, right?
MR. SACKS: Absolutely. We got to win.
THE PRESIDENT: Okay.
Thank you.
MR. SCHARF: Thank you, sir.
THE PRESIDENT: And this, David, is?
MR. SCHARF: Crypto.
MR. SACKS: Yeah, this is the crypto EO. We're going to be forming a internal working group to make crypto — to make America the world capital on crypto under your leadership.
THE PRESIDENT: Which is really going up, right?
MR. SACKS: Absolutely.
(The executive order is signed.)
THE PRESIDENT: All right, David. That's for you. (The president gives Mr. Sacks the signing pen.) Thanks.

MR. SACKS: Thank you, sir.

THE PRESIDENT: You find them exciting? They might not be exciting, but we're going to make a lot of money for the country. Okay?

MR. SACKS: Thank you, sir.

THE PRESIDENT: And so is David. You have to check him out. There is nobody like this guy. They said, "How did you get David Sacks? How did you do that?" And he's — he's doing it for the country more than anything else. So, we appreciate it, David. Thank you very much.

MR. SACKS: Thank you, sir.

MR. SCHARF: This is an executive order establishing a presidential commission — an advisory commission on science and technology.

THE PRESIDENT: Good.

(The executive order is signed.)

Do you want to explain that a little bit?

MR. SCHARF: The basic idea is to get together top people from government to private-sector technology industry, as well as educational institutions, to make sure that America maintains its leadership position with respect to science and technology development in the years ahead.

THE PRESIDENT: Good. That's great.

MR. SCHARF: Next, sir, we have a presidential memorandum encouraging departments and agencies in your government, including the Department of the Interior, to promote federal recognition of the Lumbee Tribe of —

THE PRESIDENT: Ohh.

MR. SCHARF: — North Carolina.

THE PRESIDENT: I love the Lumbee Tribe. So, this is their first big step, right?

MR. SCHARF: This would be a huge step for them, sir.

THE PRESIDENT: Yeah. They were with me all the way. They were great — North Carolina Lumbee Tribe.

(The presidential memorandum is signed.)

And we'll send — you'll send them a copy of that?

MR. SCHARF: Yes, sir.

THE PRESIDENT: They were great.

Okay?

MR. SCHARF: And, if you'd like, I could get them that pen, sir, as well.

THE PRESIDENT: Yeah, let's do that. (The president gives Mr. Scharf the signing pen.)

MR. SCHARF: Next, we have a set of pardons for peaceful pro-life protestors who were prosecuted by the Biden administration for exercising their First Amendment rights.

THE PRESIDENT: Do you know how many?

MR. SCHARF: I believe it's 23, sir.

THE PRESIDENT: Twenty-three people that were prosecuted. They should not have been prosecuted.

Man- of — many of them are — are elderly people. They should not have been prosecuted. This is a great honor to sign this.

(The proclamation is signed.)

They'll be very happy.

MR. SCHARF: Thank you, sir.

THE PRESIDENT: So, they're all in prison now?

MR. SCHARF: Some are. Some are — are out of custody.

THE PRESIDENT: It's ridiculous.

Okay?

MR. SCHARF: Lastly, sir, we have an executive order ordering the declassification of files relating to the assassinations of President John F. Kennedy, Senator Robert F. Kennedy, and the Reverend Dr. Martin Luther King, Jr.

THE PRESIDENT: That's a big one, huh? A lot of people are waiting for this for a long — for years —

MR. SCHARF: Yes, sir.

THE PRESIDENT: — for decades. And everything will be revealed.

(The executive order is signed.)

Okay. Give that to RFK, Jr. (The president gives Mr. Scharf the signing pen.)

MR. SCHARF: Yes, sir.

THE PRESIDENT: Okay.

Okay. Thank you very much.

(Cross-talk.)

Q Mr. President — Mr. President, a U.S. judge temporarily blocked the birthright citizenship order. Do you have any reaction to —

THE PRESIDENT: No. Obviously, we'll appeal it. They put it before a certain judge — in Seattle, I guess, right? And

there's no surprises with that judge.

Q Mr. President, Senators Collins and Murkowski have now said they will vote against Pete Hegseth. Are you worried about his confirmation, and your reaction?

THE PRESIDENT: No. And no surprises there. It's too bad. You know, it's the way — the way it is. Too bad.

Q And when would you adjourn Congress to make recess appointments, Mr. President?

THE PRESIDENT: Well, I'd take a look at that. I'd listen to John Thune. He's doing a fantastic job. We're moving along. The Democrats are trying to delay government, as they always do. They can't help themselves. Even John Ratcliffe, who's very, very strong, very popular and liked by the Democrats — I guess, he gets a lot of Democrat votes — that's taking a long time, and it shouldn't be taking a long time.

They — they're maxing everything out so they can delay everything as much as possible.

Q Does Senator Thune support an effort to use recess appointments if you choose to do that?

THE PRESIDENT: I'd be willing to use recess appointments. It's up to John. We'll see. John Thune is a great guy, great senator, knows his stuff inside out and backwards. But I would use recess appointments if he wants to do that. Absolutely.

(Cross-talk.)

The Democrats are just delaying. They always delay.

Q Mr. President, you spoke with the Saudi crown prince yesterday.

THE PRESIDENT: Who?

Q The Saudi crown prince.

THE PRESIDENT: Yes.

Q How was the — the call?

THE PRESIDENT: Great. It was great.

Q And they said $600 million [illegible] billion dollars they can invest?

THE PRESIDENT: Six hundred. I'll ask them for a trillion.

Q You said you're going to ask them for a trillion. Will Saudi Arabia be the first foreign country you will visit, since they're investing that much money?

THE PRESIDENT: Well, if they do that, I would, yeah.

Q You would?

THE PRESIDENT: I would be glad to do that. I

did it, as you know, four years ago. We did $450 billion — meaning the money all goes to American companies — and they purchased jets and they purchased computers and everything else. And we did $450 billion, and I guess we're at $600, $650.

(Cross-talk.)

And I'll see if I can talk them into a trillion.

Q And on the Middle East again. You showed great confidence in Steve Witkoff. Why you said that you doubt that the ceasefire in Gaza will — will hold since you appraised his efforts?

THE PRESIDENT: Well, no, I think he's great. But it's a very tricky place. It's very tricky. And we'll see. And if it — if something does happen, they will not be happy.

Q Sir, follow-up on that one. In terms of Steve Witkoff, are you going to put him in charge of — of Iran strategy? And do you want him talking directly with the Iranians?

THE PRESIDENT: No, but he — he certainly is somebody I would use. He's done a fantastic job. He's a great negotiator. He's a very good person, great — a very popular person. Gets along with people. I have great negotiators. They — they have no personality whatsoever, and then I have some that do.

Steve has a wonderful way about him and people like him. And even in this case, both sides like him, and he was able to make a deal. That deal would have never been made without Steve.

The Biden people couldn't make the deal. They were working on it for a year and a half. They couldn't make a deal. We got it done prior to the inauguration. We said it has to be before the inauguration. I mean, the deal should hold, but if it doesn't hold, there'll be a lot of problems.

(Cross-talk.)

Q Related to your AI EO. Just hours after you made that big Stargate announcement, Elon Musk tweeted that they don't actually have the money. Is that true?

THE PRESIDENT: I don't know if they do, but, you know, they're putting up the money. The government is not putting up anything. They're putting up money. They're very rich people, so I hope they do.

And, I mean, Elon doesn't like one of those people. So, (inaudible).

(Cross-talk.)

Q Are you worried that AI is going to replace many American jobs?

THE PRESIDENT: No.

Q Does that worry you?

THE PRESIDENT: No, no. It's going to create tremendous numbers of jobs. It's going to also create a lot of benefits, medically, for cancer research and other things. It's going to have a huge positive impact.

And, you know, we want to be ahead of China. We're, right now, way ahead of China.

David Sacks is one of the all-time experts. You know, that — people are amazed that he — you just met him. I don't know if he's still here.

MR. SACKS: (Inaudible.)

THE PRESIDENT: There he is.

But — but one of the most respected people in that world. It's a world. That's a whole different world.

And we're ahead of China now because of what I'm doing, and I think it's going to be very successful.

(Cross-talk.)

Q On NATO spending, please. You just asked the Davos forum again that NATO countries should spend 5 percent of GDP on defense.

THE PRESIDENT: Yeah.

Q The United States don't spend 5 percent.

THE PRESIDENT: Well, I — I don't think so, no.

Q Do you think it should also apply to the United States?

THE PRESIDENT: We're protecting them, you know? They're not protecting us. We're protecting them. So, I don't think we should be spending

— I'm not sure we should be spending anything, but we should certainly be helping them. But they should — they should up their 2 percent to 5 percent, yeah.

Q Mr. President — Mr. President, you said earlier during your speech at Davos that you would like to see interest rates come down.

THE PRESIDENT: Yeah.

Q How much would you like to see them come down?

THE PRESIDENT: A lot.

Q And will you talk with Powell?

THE PRESIDENT: I'd like to see them come down a lot, and oil prices will come down. And when oil prices come down, everything is going to be cheaper for the American people — and actually for the world — but for the American people. So, I'd like to see oil prices come down.

And when the energy comes down, that's going to knock out a lot of the inflation. That's going to automatically bring the interest rates down.

Q Are you worried that it's too much going on at once if you're —

Q Mr. President, you said that you would demand —

Q Are you worried that there's too much going on at once if you're trying to bring interest rates down and —

THE PRESIDENT: No, no.

Q — get the economy back going?

THE PRESIDENT: No. It just works that way. I mean, it just economically works that way. When the oil comes down, it'll bring down prices, then you won't have inflation, and then the interest rates will come down. (Inaudible.)

(Cross-talk.)

Q You said that you would demand that the interest rates come down.

THE PRESIDENT: Well, I would put in —

Q Do you expect —

THE PRESIDENT: I would put in a strong statement.

Q Do you expect the Fed to listen to you?

THE PRESIDENT: Yeah.

Q Are you going to talk to Powell about this and — bringing the rates down?

THE PRESIDENT: At — at the right time, I would.

Q Sir, do you plan to meet with any of the people you pardoned that were — participated in the January 6th, 2021, attack — do you plan to meet with any of them or meet with them at the White House?

THE PRESIDENT: I don't know. I'm sure that they probably would like to. I did — I did them something important. But what they did is they were protesting a crooked election. And, you know,

I mean, people understand that also. And they were treated very badly. Nobody's been treated like that. So, I'd be open to it, certainly. I — I don't know of anything like that, but I think they — they're going to — meeting some of the congresspeople — congressmen, -women —

Q Have you spoken to them?

THE PRESIDENT: — who want to — want to meet. But I'd certainly be open to it.

Q Have you spoken to them since you issued the pardons?

THE PRESIDENT: I haven't spoken to any of them yet, but I know they're very happy.

(Cross-talk.)

I gave them — I gave them their life back. Their life was taken away from them unnecessarily and unfairly. I gave them their life back. So, I can imagine they probably would like to.

Q What did you mean when you said that Biden took bad advice in not pardoning himself yesterday?

THE PRESIDENT: Well, he did. I think he did, because he — he pardoned all these people that are crooked as hell. Look, the congressmen, they're crooked. What they did is they destroyed evidence. When you destroy evidence, especially criminally like that — they did it criminally.

And the reason they destroyed the evidence is because it proved that I was right. They didn't destroy evidence for no reason. They destroyed it because they found many documents saying that I offered 10,000 soldiers. If they had 500 soldiers or National Guard, there would have been no problem. If they had 200, that would have been — I offered 10,000, if they needed them — there would have been no problem.

That's been now totally disproven. And it's also been disproven by Nancy Pelosi's daughter, who has her on tape saying it was her fault, that she has full responsibility for this.

But — and they have all that stuff. They destroyed everything, and they go through a year and a half, two years of nonsense, they come up with tremendous evidence, and they destroyed evidence.

And Schiff knew about it. That's why he's on there. He knew all about the destruction of evidence. A lot of people said he's the one that got them to do it. And he's a crooked guy — you know? — totally crooked politician. And so, he's pardoned, and some other people are pardoned.

And these are crooked politicians, every one of them. Bennie Johnson [Thompson], what he did is incredible. I mean, he was the leader of the committee, and he did it. Cheney, Crying Adam Kinzinger, all of them — they destroyed evidence and deleted everything.

There's nothing with — there's no evidence now. They're crooked politicians, and they should be punished. You know, that's — even in a civil trial, you go to jail for a thing like that. They destroyed every document, from what I understand — every document — because it proved that I was totally innocent.

Q Do you plan to send up to 10,000 troops to the southern border, sir?

THE PRESIDENT: Yeah. Oh, southern border?

Q Yes, the border.

THE PRESIDENT: When you say "southern border" — when I said "10,000 troops," I was referring to the Capitol.

Q Oh, I see. A- — and when does that —

THE PRESIDENT: No, no, you got it wrong. I was referring —

Q When do you plan

THE PRESIDENT: — to the Cap- —

Q When do you plan to do that?

THE PRESIDENT: I offered 10,000 troops to the Capitol before January 6th.

Q And as for the 1,500 at the southern border, sir, to clarify, what exactly do you want them to be doing right now?

THE PRESIDENT: Making sure that the border is safe and secure and that criminals don't come into our country.

Q Mr. President, do you think that sanctions on Russia will force President Putin to negotiate?

THE PRESIDENT: I don't know, but I think he should make a deal.

Q Mr. President, does it bother you that Elon Musk criticized a deal that you made publicly, that he said — that he tweeted that?

THE PRESIDENT: No, it doesn't. He hates one of the people in the deal. So —

Q Have you spoken to him since then?

THE PRESIDENT: No, no. I've — well, I've spoken Elon but —

Q Not about that?

THE PRESIDENT: I've spoken to all of them, actually.

No, no. The people in the deal are very, very smart people. But Elon, one of the people he happens to hate. But I have certain hatreds of people too —

Q Sir —

THE PRESIDENT: — you know?

Q Sir, on China. What do you think Xi Jinping can do on the Ukraine-Russia war?

THE PRESIDENT: Which one?

Q Ukraine-Rus- — -Russia war. What can Xi Jinping do about that?

THE PRESIDENT: China?

Q Yeah.

THE PRESIDENT: They have a lot of power over

Russia. They supply energy to Russia, and Russia supplies energy to them. They supply other things to — you know, it — it's really a very big trade. It's a very big trading partner. But Russia supplies a lot of energy to China, China pays them a lot of money for that, and I think they have a lot of power over Russia. So, I think Russia should want to make a deal.

Maybe they want to make a deal. I think, from what I hear, Putin would like to see me, and we'll meet as soon as we can. I'd — I'd meet immediately. Every day we don't meet, soldiers are being killed in a battlefield, and that battl- — battlefield is like no battlefield since World War II. That's a —

Q You said that U- — Ukraine wants to —

THE PRESIDENT: And I have — I have pictures that you don't want to see. Soldiers are being killed on a daily basis at numbers that we haven't seen in decades. And it would be nice to end that war. It's a ridiculous war.

Q You said that Ukraine is ready to make a deal. Did President Zelenskyy tell you that at — personally?

THE PRESIDENT: Yeah, sure. He's ready to negotiate a deal. He'd like to stop. He's a — he's somebody that lost a lot of soldiers, and so did Russia — lost a lot. I mean, Russia lost more soldiers. They lost 800,000 soldiers. Would you say that's a lot? I'd say it's a lot.

(Cross-talk.)

Q Mr. President, you said that you wanted to make Dr. King's dream a reality. What's your response to his children and civil rights leaders who say that your DEI orders are a contradiction of his dream and could further drive racial disparities?

THE PRESIDENT: Well, I haven't heard that.

Q Mr. President, you put the Houthis back on the terror list. How do you see the war in Yemen end now?

THE PRESIDENT: Well, we'll see what happens, but they can't shoot down our ships — the Houthis.

Q Yes.

THE PRESIDENT: And that — you can't shoot down our ships or any ships, and that's what they've been doing. So, they're on the terror list, and —

Q Mr. President —

THE PRESIDENT: — that's not good for them.

Q Mr. President —

Q Sir, why did you revoke security protections for former Secretary of State Mi- — Mike Pompeo and — and Brian Hook?

THE PRESIDENT: Well, the same reason I do — when you, you know, have protection, you can't have it for the rest of your life. Do you want to have a large detail of people guarding people for the rest of their lives? I mean, there's risks to everything.

Q Do you think a former presidents should (inaudible) —

Q Sir, would you support striking Iran's nuclear facilities?

THE PRESIDENT: Say it?

Q Would you support Israel, for example, striking Iran's nuclear facilities? Or do you —

THE PRESIDENT: Well, I'm not going to answer that.

Q — believe in diplomacy?

THE PRESIDENT: Obviously, I'm not going to answer that question. We'll have to see. I — I'm going to be meeting with various people over the next couple of days, and we'll see. But hopefully that can be worked out without having to worry about it. It would be nice — it would really be nice if that could be worked out without having to go that further step.

Q And who are you going to meet with, if I — if I may ask?

THE PRESIDENT: Well, I'd rather not say that, but very high-level people. But hopefully that could be worked out.

You know, look, Iran, hopefully, will be — make a deal. And if they don't make a deal, I guess that's okay too.

Q And, Mr. President, just to follow up, you said you think the Fed should listen to you. Can you elaborate on why you think it should?

THE PRESIDENT: With regard to interest rates?

Q Correct, yes.

THE PRESIDENT: Because I think I know interest rates much better than they do, and I think I know it certainly much better than the one who's primarily in charge of making that decision.

But, no, I'm guided by them very much, but if I disagree, I will let it be known.

Q Mr. President —

Q Sir, your tariffs planned for China and Mexico are much tougher — or the ones for Canada and Mexico are much tougher than the one for China. Why is it softer for China?

THE PRESIDENT: Well, China is already paying a lot of tariffs because of me, and when you add them up, I would say, you know, they're paying a lot. They paid hundreds of billions of dollars. They never paid 10 cents until I came along. When I came along, they pay hundreds of — they've paid hundreds of billions of dollars. Never paid anything. And so, they've already started at a higher base.

Q Is February 1st —

Q Sir, about the border —

Q — the date for Chinese tariffs as well, sir? February 1? Or was that just Mexico and Canada?

THE PRESIDENT: It's Mexico and Canada. But

we'll — we're talking about China too. Look, China is sending us tremendous amounts of bad drugs: fentanyl — really bad stuff. Most of it comes through Mexico. And we're losing, I s- — I think, 300,000 lives a year because of that. People say 150, 100, 120. I think 300,000 lives a year. Those are old numbers. The other — the lower number is a low number. And we can't have that. They've got to stop sending it.

I had a deal with President Xi, but it was a deal that wasn't followed up by Biden, of course, where they were going to issue the death penalty to people that make fentanyl, and that would have stopped it. But we'll have to stop it with tariffs.

Okay? Thank you very much, everybody.

Q So, is China (inaudible) —

(Cross-talk.)

THE PRESIDENT: Thank you. Thank you. Thank you very much. Appreciate it.

Q Thank you, Mr. President.

THE PRESIDENT: Thank you.

END 3:30 P.M. EST

## Remarks by President Trump after Air Force One Arrival Fletcher, NC

### January 24, 2025

REMARKS BY PRESIDENT TRUMP

AFTER AIR FORCE ONE ARRIVAL
Asheville Regional Airport
Fletcher, North Carolina
11:07 A.M. EST

THE PRESIDENT: Well, thank you very much. Everybody thought I was going to California. I said, "No, no. I'm stopping in North Carolina first, because they've been abused by what's happened." I mean, it's terrible. It should have been done. It should have been — a lot of things should have happened that didn't happen. So, we're here. We're going to fix it out.

We're working with the gentleman behind me, and you know who they are. And we're going to fix it, and we're going to fix it as fast as you can. It's a massive amount of damage. FEMA has really let us down, let the country down. And I don't know if that's Biden's fault or whose fault it is, but we're going to take over, and we're going to do a good job.

We're going to assign Mr. Whatley — who's fantastic, frankly — and the governor and everybody else that's going to work. We're going to supply the money — we'll supply a lot of the money. Maybe you have to chip in something — you'll chip in a little something, like —

GOVERNOR STEIN: We will.

THE PRESIDENT: — maybe 25 percent or whatever.

But we're going to get it done as quickly as we can, and we want to take care of the people of North Carolina.

It's so interesting. Everybody is talking about California, and that's a mess. But I said, "I'm not going to California until I stop in North Carolina." So, here we are.

We're going to go visit the site, and we're going to work with probably three of the congressmen — Republican congressmen — who've been fantastic — whose areas have been affected, and with Michael Whatley, the governor, and whoever else is — you know, we decide to get involved.

Probably less FEMA, because FEMA just hasn't done the job. And we're looking at the whole concept of FEMA. I like, frankly, the concept: When North Carolina gets hit, the governor takes care of it. When Florida gets hit, the governor takes care of it, meaning the state takes care of it.

To have a group of people come in from an area that don't even know where they're going in order to solve immediately a problem is something that never worked for me. But this is probably one of the best examples of it not working.

And there's been some others, like in Louisiana, et cetera. So, we're going to be doing something on FEMA that I think most people agree.

I'd like to see the states take care of disasters. Let the state take care of the tornadoes and the hurricanes and all of the other things that happen. And I think you're going to find it a lot less expensive. You'll do it for less than half, and you're going to get a lot quicker response.

So, that seems to be the recommendation, but we'll be making that recommendation over the next couple of weeks.

We're going to go to the site now, and we're going to figure out a plan — a plan for really demolition and cleaning, because not a lot has been done. And we're very disappointed in the Biden administration, but we're going to make up for lost time. And I said I'd do that, and this is about the earliest we could possibly be here, and we're honored to be here. This has been a great state. They're great people, and they've really been mishandled. But it's all — this group is going to be great, and we're going to get it taken care of.

Any questions?

Q How — how will you respond —

Q How will you make those changes to FEMA? Do you do you expect to ask Congress for additional aid for North Carolina and California?

THE PRESIDENT: Yeah, it will be direct. In other words, the aid will go through us. So, rather than going through FEMA, it will go through us. And

I think maybe this is a good place to start, because — and in all fairness to the governor, in all fairness to everybody else, FEMA was not on the ball, and we're going to turn it all around.

Yes.

Q A lot — a lot of Americans think that this is symbolic of what your campaign was all about: America first, putting your prior- — priorities to Americans, even going to California, where their policies might mo- — have been one of the biggest reasons why they've had these problems. But you're putting the American people first. Your thoughts on that?

THE PRESIDENT: We are. We're puttin- — thank you. I like that question. Boy, I want more questions like that. That's even a statement. Thank you very much.

Q Thank you.

THE PRESIDENT: He's a good man, that guy, and he's also a very professional reporter, I have to say. Thank you very much.

Q You're welcome.

THE PRESIDENT: Yeah, we're putting America first. We're putting, in this case, North Carolina and California — we're going to do a good job in California. That is a disaster like — I don't know if we've ever seen anything like it, frankly. They say "the biggest in the history of California." I think

— has anything bigger than that happened in the whole country ever? It looks like — I don't want to say what it looks like, but you know what I'm going to say. It looks like something hit it.

Q Yeah.

THE PRESIDENT: And we won't talk about what hit it, but it is a bad, bad situation.

And I guess I'm going to meet with some government officials, but, I mean, much more importantly — and in California, just to revert to it for a second, millions of gallons of water are waiting to be poured down through already the half pipes that are already built. I mean, they've been up for 40 years. And about 20 years ago, they turned off the water. And it's the water that comes from the Pacific Northwest — some of it comes out of Canada — and it flows there, and it probably has flowed there for a million years. And they turned it off, and they route out to the Pacific.

And in the meantime, you don't have water in the hydrants. You don't have water in the sprinkler systems. It's the craziest thing I've ever seen.

And everyone's trying to figure out: Why aren't they turning it back? They say it's the delta smelt — it's a fish — but I find that hard to believe. But we'll —

Q Mr. President, what you are —

THE PRESIDENT: — figure it out. And without

— and without doing that, you're going to continue to have problems.

Q Mr. President, what are you prepared to do, sir, if OPEC doesn't respond to your call to cut oil prices?

THE PRESIDENT: Well, we want to see OPEC cut the price of oil, and that will automatically stop the tragedy that's taking place in Ukraine. It's a butchering tragedy for both sides, by the way. A tremendous number of Russian soldiers are dead; a tremendous number of Ukrainian soldiers, and a lot of people are dead from the bombing of the cities.

But right now, it's just bullets whacking and hitting men — mostly men — almost in all cases, men. And they're — over a million men are killed, and they're lo- — they're losing thousands of people a week. It's crazy.

It's a crazy war, and it never would have happened if I was president. Would never have happened. This is crazy that it happened, but we want to stop it.

Now, one way to stop it quickly is for OPEC to stop making so much money and to drop the price of oil, because they have it nice and high. And if you have it high, that war is not going to end so easily.

So, OPEC ought to get on the ball, and they ought

to drop the price of oil, and that war will stop right away.

Q Will you withhold funding to Los Angeles because of its sanctuary city policy?

THE PRESIDENT: I want to see two things in Los Angeles: Voter ID, so that the people have a chance to vote, and I want to see the water be released and come down into Los Angeles and throughout the state. Those are the two things.

After that, I will be the greatest president that California have ever — has ever seen.

Q Will there —

THE PRESIDENT: I want the water to come down and come down to Los Angeles and also go out to all the farmland that's barren and dry.

You know, they have land that they say is the equivalent of the land in Iowa, which is about as good as there is anywhere on Earth. The problem is it's artificial, because they artificially stop the water from going on to the land.

So, I want two things. I want voter ID for the people of California, and they all want it. Right now, you have no — you don't have voter ID. People want to have voter identification. You want to have proof of citizenship. Ideally, you have one-day voting, but I just want voter ID as a start. And I want the water to be released, and they're going to get a lot of help from the U.S.

Thank you very much. I'll see you in a little while.
Q Will there be (inaudible) —
THE PRESIDENT: We'll see you at the site.
Q Will there —
Q Thank you, sir.
THE PRESIDENT: We'll see you at the site.
Q Can you tell us more about the deportation flights? Where are they going from? Where —
THE PRESIDENT: It's going very well.
Q — are they going to?
THE PRESIDENT: Deportation is going very well. We're getting the bad, hard criminals out. These are murderers. These are people that have been as bad as you get, as bad as anybody you've seen. We're taking them out first.
Thank you.

## Remarks by President Trump during tour of Hurricane Helene Disaster Site

### January 24, 2025 12:39 P.M. EST

Private Residence Asheville, North Carolina
THE PRESIDENT: Thank you very much, Franklin. Thank you. A good man. He's done a great job, a fantastic job.
And we've come to North Carolina with a simple message for all the people of this region who

were hit so hard by Hurricane Helene. And that message is very simple: You are not forgotten any longer. You were treated very badly by the previous administration. And I'm here after a few days of the administration.

We're going to California, Los Angeles. They got hit hard, as you know. A lot of that could have been prevented, I think, if they had water, which they had plenty of, but they didn't use it.

But I'm going there, but — and it was set up to go there, and I said, "Well, wait a minute, what about North Carolina?"

They said, "Well, what." I said, "I have to stop there first. I'm stopping in North Carolina."

So, we made the stop, and I feel very good. You're represented by some great people. Great, great congressmen are with us, and we're going to get involved with them.

And Michael Whatley is here, who is the head of the Republican Party. He worked with Lara Trump to take us through to a tremendous victory, one of the — as the media says, one of the most consequential presidential elections ever — they say in 129 years, whatever that may mean.

But whatever it is, it was a great election we had, and we won your state. All three times, we won your state. And all three primaries, we won your state. So, we won it six times, I guess, Mr. Congressman, huh?

And it's a great place. And I wanted to come here and before I went anywhere, frankly.

In the campaign, I promised that I'd come back to western North Carolina to help the people of the state. And today, here I am to deliver on that promise. And we have a lot of things in mind, and we're getting the Army Corps of Engineers all set. You need your riverbanks fixed. You need a lot of roads fixed. And we're going to get it done in rapid time.

And I've asked Susie Wiles and all of my people to start calling up and get the Corps ready, and they're going to get ready to go. I don't know what it is — I don't know what took so long for the other administration.

But remember, I wasn't here for the first four months or three months, whatever it may be. You, we can only start as of, essentially, one or two days ago. And we've made a lot of progress over the last couple of days, Michael.

I understand we're going to get you the resources you need and the support that you deserve, and we'll be at your side through every step of the rebuilding. And no American is going to be left behind. The people that I just met are so great, and the people that own that house is going to be very beautiful in a little while. And who knows, if Franklin decides, maybe he'll rip it down and build them a new one, because sometimes he can do that just as easily. But we're going to take care of the people.

I want to thank our great first lady for coming today. She really wanted to be here. She said, "No, I want to go." And, you know, she sees what happened and she felt very badly, and she wanted to go. And we're then going out together to Los Angeles, but she wanted to be in North Carolina. She saw what happened. She has a — she has a feeling like I do for North Carolina.

So, thanks, as well, to a great gentleman, Franklin Graham. And his father, Billy Graham — I used to go with my father to Yankee Stadium and places to watch his father preach. And he was some preacher. Where is he — he was some — you got good stock. You come from the ultimate genes, I can tell you. But he was really something.

And Franklin, though, has done so much, and his father is looking down on him right now, I guarantee you. For a long time, he's been looking down on Franklin, saying, "I'm very proud of you, son." He really is, because what Franklin has done with Samaritan's Purse is incredible. They told me just yesterday that Samaritan's Purse has been great.

But the FEMA people sort of left you high and dry, but we're going to change that around. We're not happy with FEMA.

As well as all of the representatives — you have great representatives here. Chuck Edwards, who's here someplace. Where is Chuck?

PARTICIPANT: Right here.

THE PRESIDENT: Where is Chuck? Chuck?

Tim Moore. Tim — thank you, Tim. Great job too, both of you guys.

Virginia Foxx, a power — she's a power, that one. Don't — don't ever have her as your enemy. It's not good. (Laughter.) It's not healthy.

Pat Harrigan. Good job, Pat.

Addison McDowell. These guys were just here, just put in, and they're doing a fantastic job. Addison, thank you very much. Great.

Mark Harris. Thank you, Mark. Thank you, Mark.

Brad Knott. Thank you, Brad.

Greg Murphy, a fantastic guy — my friend for a long time now, right?

REPRESENTATIVE MURPHY: Yes, sir.

THE PRESIDENT: And the RNC chairman, Michael Whatley, who really, as I said, brought us to a great victory with Lara the chairman of the party, the whole Republican — I took Michael Whatley from North Carolina, because he did the best job, and put him in charge of everything. And the job they did together was incredible.

Last September, Hurricane Helene became one of the deadliest natural disasters in modern American history. Rainfall rose to far more than 30 inches, which is lethal, unleashing unprecedented devastation throughout western North Carolina and many other states, as you know, but you got hit the hardest.

The highest responsibility and deepest obligation of the American government is to protect its people, and that's never truer than in times of emergency like this. Unfortunately, our government failed you, but it wasn't the Trump government. It was a government run by Biden. What a terrible situation. But our government failed the people of North Carolina in this horrible crisis.

For two months, Asheville lacked running water. And even today, some North Carolinians can't take a hot-water shower. They can't drink water. They don't know where to get it. They have to — it's delivered to them by somewhere. They just go out and somehow find some.

It's been four months since the storm made landfill [landfall], and still 180 roads remain closed and in ruins. Earlier this month, the Biden administration kicked 2,000 displaced North Carolinians out of their temporary housing into freezing, 20-degree weather — I don't know how they did that one, because it was cold — even while your government provided shelter and housing for illegal aliens from all over the world.

But under the Trump administration, the days of betrayal and neglect are over. They are over.

As I said in my Inaugural Address, we restore the integrity, competency, and loyalty of the American government. And I think I said most of it in the Inaugural Address. We said a lot of things, but one of the groups of people I was thinking about is you in North Carolina. A lot of that was in reference to you and what you've had to suffer.

I'm pleased to announce that under our leadership, the federal government will be surging housing solutions to the state that go beyond mere temporary hotel stays that ended up being very short term. The government wouldn't do it any longer, which is ridiculous.

We'll marshal all available resources that bring back potable water and make your water and infrastructure dramatically more reliable very quickly.

And today, I'll also be signing an executive order slashing all red tape and bureaucratic barriers and permits to ensure the rapid reconstruction of the roads here in western North Carolina. We're going to go through a permitting process that's called "No permitting. Just get it done." That's the way they built them many years ago, I guarantee you that. Right?

We will get them back very quickly. And we'll begin the work of funderv- — fundamentally changing, terminating, or overhauling FEMA. FEMA has been a disaster, no matter where they are.

We're honored to be joined today, very quickly, by several families affected by the vicious storm. I'd like to ask each of them to share their story. Chris and Kim West, you can come forward. Ramona Nix, Jackie Mitchell, and Thomas Gary Bright, and finally, the Wright family. And come on up and maybe say a few words. Please. Thank you very much.

Hello.

MS. WEST: Hi.

THE PRESIDENT: Come on in here.

MS. WEST: (Laughs.) Whenever it started, we started moving our vehicles to the top of the road. And by the time we got the vehicles moved, the water had already hit our ankles in the house. And so, I grabbed my purse and my little pug dog, and my husband grabbed the dog food and put it in a trash bag. And by the time we got out into the driveway, it was already waist deep, and there was sticks and that kind of thing.

I didn't think I was going to make it, but we did make it out, and we made it to the top of the road. And we were kind of stuck there for hours because we couldn't get out any other ways, because it was flooded all the way around. It took us hours, and we sat there.

And finally, it receded enough to where we could actually get out. It was probably, like, close to midnight. And it started like, 5, 6 o'clock in the morning.

We just lost everything that we had. Didn't even have a brush for, like, three days. So —

THE PRESIDENT: Thank you. Come on over.

MS. WEST: Thank you.

MR. WEST: That —

THE PRESIDENT: Okay.

Would you like to say something with that beautiful baby?

MR. WRIGHT: Say, "hey."

Yeah. So, when the hurricane storms hit North Carolina, hit our home, my daughter and my wife and I were actually out of town. But unfortunately, my dad, who was still home, and my mother was staying at our house with our [illegible] with our animals.

And my — the waters got so high that it actually lifted — between that and the tornado that came through — or microburst is what they've been calling them — and lifted his home and the house that I grew up in and crashed it into our barn. It took away his business. It took away all of our tools and tractors and everything needed to keep the farm going.

And my mother was trapped in the house, and there was no way to escape because the water got so high.

The only thing she could do was ride it out and wait until the waters came down.

So, we've been doing a little bit of battling with our insurance and FEMA. We did have proper insurance, with flood insurance and homeowner's insurance, but since we had proper insurance, FEMA has not been able to assist us with a whole lot of things.

And, again, we've been having some issues with trying to get some payout for our insurance in a timely manner. We had to do mold mitigation on our home, which is extremely expensive, before the structural engineer even came out in order to get our flood payout. And to me, that was not really acceptable.

THE PRESIDENT: Has the insurance company been responsive, or not really?

MR. WRIGHT: Not — not so much. You know, again —

THE PRESIDENT: Are they going to give you they have to give you? Huh?

MR. WRIGHT: I'm — I'm hoping so.

THE PRESIDENT: (Inaudible.)

MR. WRIGHT: And we might need — I mean, we need some assistance with that. We reached out to an attorney.

THE PRESIDENT: What's the name of the insurance company?

MR. WRIGHT: North Carolina Farm Bureau.

THE PRESIDENT: You've got a mortgage, right?

MR. WRIGHT: Yep.

THE PRESIDENT: That's terrible.

MR. WRIGHT: That's what we're after here. So —

THE PRESIDENT: Are a lot of people having that problem too with the insurance companies, general? Different insurance companies? And they're all difficult, or just the one particular one?

MR. WRIGHT: I've heard different stories from others, and a lot of folks are —

THE PRESIDENT: Have you heard some were responsive, that some were good?

MR. WRIGHT: I've heard some — some good instances of even Farm Bureau themselves. But in my case, you know, they'd sent out a third-party adjuster immediately. Well, they wound up firing that third-party adjuster group. He gave us a quote for a much higher estimate than what we received.

THE PRESIDENT: And he got fired?

MR. WRIGHT: And then he got let go. Yeah, he got fired. So, then they brought in another third-party adjuster to come in and lowball us.

We've not received any kind of — so, the flood insurance is our primary insurance. And so, there was roof leaks in the home that the inspectors found — the adjusters. Well, that contributed to us losing some of our personal property, as it come in the third story, where there's no — or second-story living space, where the flood wa- — well above the flood waters. So, they've neglected us for —

THE PRESIDENT: Was your mother saved?

MR. WRIGHT: Yes, yes, she was saved.

THE PRESIDENT: (Inaudible.)

MR. WRIGHT: She's right here.

THE PRESIDENT: Oh, good. Okay. You made it.

MR. WRIGHT: So, we — yeah, we made it.

THE PRESIDENT: That was not exciting, right?

MR. WRIGHT: That's right.

THE PRESIDENT: How scared were you?

MS. WRIGHT: Very.

THE PRESIDENT: Did you think you were going to make it?

MS. WRIGHT: No.

THE PRESIDENT: You didn't think so?

MS. WRIGHT: Nope. I just started praying.

THE PRESIDENT: So, you were sort of on a boat? Your house became a boat, huh?

MS. WRIGHT: (Laughs.)

MR. WRIGHT: It's a big pontoon.

THE PRESIDENT: Wow. That's some story. Would you like to say something?

MR. WRIGHT: It was a beach house on — on the steps.

THE PRESIDENT: I'll bet this guy would like to say something, I can tell.

MR. WRIGHT: I was next door to the house, and my son was out of town. So, when he came in to Charlotte — to my sister's, he called about 2:00 in the morning, because at midnight, the water was still in the stream.

THE PRESIDENT: Right. (Inaudible.)

MR. WRIGHT: In — within the banks. So, when he called, the water was coming up. So, I started moving vehicles up to about 5:30 in the morning. And she was in the house, and I pulled up to the steps, and I said, "Hop on the fender, and I'll get you out." Well, it — he built a beach house on stilts —

THE PRESIDENT: Right.

MR. WRIGHT: — five times higher than the floodplain.

And she said, "Well, he said I'd be okay."

THE PRESIDENT: Right.

MR. WRIGHT: "So, I'm staying with the dogs."

THE PRESIDENT: Right.

MR. WRIGHT: So, I went to higher ground with some vehicles, hers included, and the water covered everything. But I'd already seen it coming around both sides of my place, so I got my blind and deaf dog and a bag of valuables and took up off the side of the hill behind my house. And then was head-

ing to the cemetery back there because I knew it was open, because there was trees falling —
THE PRESIDENT: Right.
MR. WRIGHT: — and right uprooting. It was raining. I mean, it was —
THE PRESIDENT: You never saw anything like that before?
MR. WRIGHT: No, no. I've been through floods —
THE PRESIDENT: There's never been anything like that before.
MR. WRIGHT: — all my life around here. Never, no.
THE PRESIDENT: Never been anything like it.
MR. WRIGHT: Mm-hmm. Mm-hmm.
THE PRESIDENT: But you've okay, right?
MR. WRIGHT: Yep.
THE PRESIDENT: All right. Come here.
MR. WRIGHT: House is destroyed.
THE PRESIDENT: Yeah, well, we're going to help you out there. We're going to help you out.
MR. WRIGHT: Appreciate you.
THE PRESIDENT: That's what we're here for.
MR. WRIGHT: Thanks for being here.
THE PRESIDENT: Anybody else? You guys okay? Please. Please.
MR. BRIGHT: Our day that morning began — I'm a little taller — with some trees falling into our

house, which our house is — goes back four generations, 80 years, and never came close to flooding. And we woke up with trees about 4:30 or 5:00 in the morning.

And our house sits three tenths of a mile back off the road. And the water — you know, we've had flooding and such in the lake, but nothing like we saw. And like most everybody else, we moved five vehicles as far up — lawnmowers and everything else. And the water started coming in the house.

And when it got up to about ankle high, we have a loft. I got her up in that and tried to gather what you might want, which was totally random. And when it made it to the loft and started getting up to about our hips, I built a little makeshift ladder, and we got out on our roof. And we spent four hours on the roof. I had a little baggie. I — I di- — I did notes on my cell phone to my two kids and my two grandkids and something to identify me, in case we were lost in it.

THE PRESIDENT: Did you think you were going to make it?

MR. BRIGHT: No. We — we're —

THE PRESIDENT: Oh, you didn't think so?

MR. BRIGHT: Yeah, we didn't think we were going to make it at all. I mean, our house was 25 feet underwater. And —

THE PRESIDENT: So, you didn't think you were

going to live?

MR. BRIGHT: No, we were watching houses, trailers, bodies coming by us. And we live in the Azalea Road area of — in East Asheville. Oteen.

MS. MITCHELL: We watched our garage lift up and float away.

MR. BRIGHT: Yeah, we watched our garage float by.

THE PRESIDENT: It just lift up?

MR. BRIGHT: Yeah.

But, you know, we — we got to a point where it crested about four feet up on the roof. We took about three or four hours for it so it could kind of do everything in reverse and got out in the mud to higher ground. And I got out — higher ground, up toward the Subway and got over to her daughter's house, where — when she saw that I didn't have her, she lost it. And I was like, "She's okay. She's alive." And we tried to make our way back in there and gather things best we could.

But, you know, found a body right away. We had — there was about eight bodies in our area that first two weeks, located. And we were lucky we weren't one of them and — and blessed.

But like other people, no insurance on flood insurance, so we — we had to depend on FEMA. They did what they could do. And, of course, it's not enough.

THE PRESIDENT: Yeah, no, I know. (Inaudible.)
MR. BRIGHT: Yeah. Yeah. Yeah.
THE PRESIDENT: (Inaudible.)
MR. BRIGHT: Yeah, no, it's crazy.
But, yeah, again, we're thankful to be alive, but it's a long haul.
THE PRESIDENT: So, what are you doing now?
MR. BRIGHT: Staying in a camper. I've never been — if you all have noticed, I'm a big guy. I don't sleep in campers very — (laughter) — very well. And the — the first night we spent in the camper — very grateful with the Asheville Dream Center coming through with one and —
THE PRESIDENT: Do you still have the land?
MR. BRIGHT: Oh, yeah. It's — it's family land. Yeah, the land, it looks like a beach now; it's sand.
MS. MITCHELL: Yeah.
MR. BRIGHT: But —
THE PRESIDENT: Can it be built on?
MR. BRIGHT: Yes.
THE PRESIDENT: Do you intend to do that?
MR. BRIGHT: Yes.
THE PRESIDENT: You want to build again?
MR. BRIGHT: Yeah, Samaritan's Purse — we're working with them. We're working with people. We — you know, it's — it's 80 years, four generations.

THE PRESIDENT: But the house is totally gone?

MR. BRIGHT: No, the house is there. It's down to —

MS. MITCHELL: They — they gutted it to just the rafters.

MR. BRIGHT: Yeah, they came in and mudded it, but everything in it was completely destroyed. But, yeah, it's — it's tough. I think we're at a point in Asheville where peoples forgot about Asheville and —

THE PRESIDENT: (Inaudible.)

MR. BRIGHT: It's — it's stag- — everything is stopped.

THE PRESIDENT: (Inaudible.)

MR. BRIGHT: Yeah. Yeah. Thank you, sir. Appreciate that.

THE PRESIDENT: We're going to take care of you.

MR. BRIGHT: Thank you, Jackie.

MS. MITCHELL: Thank you.

THE PRESIDENT: Thank you.

MS. MITCHELL: Thank you. Stay well.

THE PRESIDENT: Thank you. Please

MS. NIX: I'm Pastor Nix. Our church is right down the road. We had only purchased in May, and it's a big church. We're a small congregation. And I had people say, "What are you going to do with this big building?" And I said, "Only God knows."

And we had our dedication, and the storm came the next week.

And the outpouring of people — my son brought the first load of supplies. And from there, I stayed there for about three months. I slept on the floor for about three weeks because the need was so great. The people were so devastated.

And I said, "I want to be here for them." And they were coming in just day and night, so there's really no need for me to go home.

But we had people from Kentucky, Tennessee, Texas, Indiana, Oklahoma — people from all over. We have not received any help — like, from the government — anything. But I said, "Lord, if you want us to do that" —

THE PRESIDENT: (Inaudible) helped you?

MS. NIX: People.

THE PRESIDENT: So, they came from all over the —

MS. NIX: All over the states.

MR. BRIGHT: (Inaudible) groups, that's what — that's what did it.

THE PRESIDENT: But FEMA — FEMA did nothing, right?

MS. NIX: No.

MR. BRIGHT: It was the — it was the — the locals.

THE PRESIDENT: FEMA is a waste of time and

money.

MS. NIX: The locals and the people that — that knew us.

And before the week was over, our church was so packed with supplies, we couldn't even — we couldn't even walk. Even in our sanctuary, it was up to the platform —

THE PRESIDENT: That's great.

MS. NIX: — of things, and in our halls and in our rooms. And we're just now beginning to get a little straightened out.

But somebody said, "How long are you going to be here?" I said, "I'm going to be here through the winter and even on, if possible," because when you meet people that's been through this struggle — I had a little lady come up, and I said, "Can we do anything special for you?" And she said, "I don't want to be selfish," but said, "Could I have a cup of coffee?" And I handed her that coffee, and she stood there, and tears just poured.

She said, "You don't realize how — how important the — the little things." It's not the big things in life that we have, but it's the little things and — and knowing that God is our source. I don't look to man. I don't have to have a lot of things. I — I had trees — about 20 trees down in my yard, but that didn't really matter. It doesn't matter, because the needs of the people is what — is what I want to be there for.

And God is good.

THE PRESIDENT: He's very good.

MS. NIX: He's very good.

And my daughter — now, she — her house is really in bad shape. And I'll let her tell you about that.

THE PRESIDENT: Okay.

MS. NIX: But thank you, President.

THE PRESIDENT: Thank you very much.

MS. NIX: This is our president.

THE PRESIDENT: (Laughs.)

MS. NIX: We appreciate you so much.

THE FIRST LADY: Thank you. Thank you all. Thank you. Thank for all what you do.

MS. NIX-ROPER: I live out in the Fairview area of North Carolina and the — near the Bat Cave, Lake Lure area, and our area was hit — it was hit really hard. I [illegible] I was home alone, and my husband had stayed in town because we take care of a little lady that's 98 years old, and she lives out in the woods by herself. And I said, "Just stay with her and make sure that she's okay."

And I got up the next morning, and my first thought was, "I want to go see what our road and bridge looks like."

So, as I was making it down to the road and the bridge, there was no road and bridge. And so, you know, here we are. We're, like, in a little island.

You know, we can't access the main road or anything.

And then the fire department came by the next day and said that they were evacuating me and my neighbor because a landslide was going to come, and they told me to get my stuff and get ready.

And so, while I was getting my stuff and getting ready, there was a knock at the door. So, I thought it was the fireman. And I went to the door, and there stood my 21-year-old son — his name is Nathan — and he had drove as far as he could to get to me. But he hiked five miles, and it took him a really long time. And he got there, and he said — he said, "Mom, grab a bag. We got to go." And I said, "Son, there's no way I can — I can hike out of here." And he's like, "No." He said, "We got to go."

So, we — we started hiking out, and I — and I seen one of my neighbors who — she had no clothes on. Her — her — she was — her skin was — was, like, chunked up. It was just — she was blue. She had been — she had been in the — in the waters. And where she had went or — or — I don't know, but it — horrific, is just all I can say.

But then, as — as me and my son hiked on out, we went through where this — this place — we call it Craigtown — but there were, like, a lot of family members there that passed away — like 11 of them. And — and there — there were people out everywhere looking for their loved ones. And there were — there were dead bodies, you know? My son's like, "Mom, you're going to see things you don't want to see."

And so, anyway, we got through all that, but I stayed at our church in our sound booth. My husband and I, we just slept up in the sound booth for a couple of months because we didn't have power or anything for about two months out there.

And then we — we have went back. I've been fighting with FEMA since day one.

Our community — there's, like, 32 homes. We don't have a road and a bridge. We're driving through our neighbors' property. You know, I went to EMS, and I said, "Look, my concern is, if we have a fire or we have an emergency out here, you're not going to get to us. You can't get those big trucks up here."

And — and I've called and called and called FEMA. And, you know, I said it's — this happened on September 27th. That's four months ago. Well, for us, today is still September 27th. You know, we haven't had help.

And so, when I talk to FEMA, I'm explaining the road and the bridge, and they send me a letter that tells me to — to basically fix it and send in my receipts, and they'll refund me some money. I'm looking at a road and bridge that, honestly, the bridge itself is probably going to be $300,000, and the road could be close to that also, because we have to have — the community has to have big boulders brought in. We're not a rich community. We can't fix it ourself.

You know, it's just — and as far as, like, house repairs, I'm still pending. I can't get money from FEMA until I fix the road and bridge and fen- — and send in my — my proof that it's fixed and everything. It's — it's just — it's been a nightmare. And I totally feel like — that we have been forgotten.

If it had not been for — for our fellow American citizens who stepped up to help us, I don't know what we would have done. I have — I have five neighbors around me who completely lost everything. You know, I have damage to my house and — and I feel — I don't feel entitled. I'm embarrassed to even say I need help, because, you know — and sometimes there's even that — that survivors' guilt, is what they're calling it. But you feel guilty to even be alive sometimes, you know, when you look around and you see your neighbors that are gone.

And it's just, you know — we — we need help. I wrote a letter that — to send to Congress. You know, "I don't understand what's going on. If we can't get FEMA help, then will you guys help us? Will you step up and be our fellow citizen? Will you step up and be our neighbor and send us something. Help us. Help us get our community back." It's — I could go on. It's just a — I don't know, it's just heartbreaking.

I appreciate you.

THE PRESIDENT: Thank you.

A good daughter you have, huh? A good daughter. Take care of mom. And your son must be great.

MS. NIX-ROPER: My son is great.

THE PRESIDENT: No, he sounds like a real leader and smart.

MS. NIX-ROPER: He really is. Th- — to hike in —

THE PRESIDENT: So, how would you have been if he didn't come and get you?

MS. NIX-ROPER: I don't know. I'd — I'd just been — would have been there until — because the only thing we could do — there were no way to get out there. The only thing we could do is just hike up to the church, the first church that was up there — about three miles to — to get, you know, maybe what we needed —

THE PRESIDENT: You tell him he's just —

MS. NIX-ROPER: — or some — I don't know.

THE PRESIDENT: Tell him he's a real leader.

MS. NIX-ROPER: He is. Thank you.

THE PRESIDENT: Sounds good.

Well, again, thank you very much, everybody.

So, we're going to be here. We're going to be working with our congressmen and woman, and they're going to do a job. And Michael Whatley is going to be very much in charge, and you'll get it done.

And FEMA is ready to rock. They haven't done the job, because they weren't really told to do the job by Biden. I guess Biden was thinking about other things, wasn't he? But they weren't told.

What they did to — what the past administration did to North Carolina is a disgrace.

So, I just want to wish you all well. I was here right after the event, and I couldn't believe it. I have never seen anything like it. I've seen a lot of bad things, but I've never seen anything like it.

And it's an honor to meet the people behind me, and it's an honor to be with our congressional delegation and some of the other politicians in the area. And it's an honor to have Michael Whatley at my side, because maybe we wouldn't be standing here as president if he wasn't.

Him and Lara — Lara Trump — were unbelievable as the head of the Republican Party. So, he happens to come from a place called North Carolina. So, I said, "Michael, fix it." (Laughs.) So, good luck. Good luck.

And we'll supply what you need. You know that. Okay? Thank you.

Thank you all very much. Thank you very much.

Q Mr. President, what kind of role will Mr. Whatley have?

Q Mr. President, I'm hearing all these heartbreaking stories and how there's been so many local groups —

THE PRESIDENT: Yeah.

Q — who have stepped up to —

THE PRESIDENT: Yeah.

Q — assist these families.

THE PRESIDENT: That's one of the things you hear.

Q Is there any talk on having money — instead of going to FEMA and going through the bureaucracy — to go through them?

THE PRESIDENT: Yeah, that's what I want to do. We want to bring it locally so that a state takes care of its problem, and then they can bring it down to a local level, like Samaritan's Purse and Franklin, because that's, you know, one of the better examples. But you had numbers of people that did a great job. You have groups that did a great job and organizations.

The one that didn't do a good job was the government. They did a bad job. They did in many ways, they did no job. They weren't even available.

So, good question. The answer is: We go local. I think it will work much better.

FEMA is a very expensive organization that really doesn't work out very well. It hasn't. This is not the only example.

So, if it was up to me right now, I'd end it right now, and I'd just let the state take care of the problem. I mean, you're going to always have problems. Let the state — if it's Florida, it's a hurricane, let Florida take care of it. They don't need FEMA to come in.

Yeah.

Q What kind of role do you envision for Mr. Whatley? Is it within FEMA, outside of FEMA?

THE PRESIDENT: Yeah, I envision a very important role for him. It's any role he wants. He's a very capable guy. Michael Whatley, a very capable guy. And he's friends and works with these guys. Keeps them elected, right? They have to do a good job. Otherwise, no matter how good Michael is, not going to work. But they've done an amazing job. They've been great.

You're lucky. You have great congressmen here and — and -woman, by the way — a great woman, very powerful woman. And they're going to do a great job. They'll do it together. They'll work together, and we'll supply what they need as they need it. We'll coordinate that.

And we will immediately get the Army Corps, Michael, because you need roads built. You know, we're talking about the bridge, we're talking about roads and things, so we've got to get them built.

All right? Okay?

Thank you all very much. Thank you very much.

END 1:10 P.M. EST

## Press Gaggle by President Trump aboard Air Force One

### January 25, 2025 3:07 P.M. MST

Aboard Air Force One En Route Miami, Florida

Q Welcome back, Mr. President.

THE PRESIDENT: Hello, everybody. How are you?

Q Welcome back.

THE PRESIDENT: Welcome back to you.

Q How are you liking Air Force One so far, sir?

THE PRESIDENT: I think it's nice. Hasn't changed.

Q Yeah.

THE PRESIDENT: Hasn't changed very much.

How's everything going? Good? Everybody happy?

Q Yes, very much so.

THE PRESIDENT: You're getting a little bit more access to your president than you did the last time, slightly — like, by about 5,000 percent. (Laughter.)

We had a very good week — first week. Almost complete. I guess one day is left, if you think about it. We're heading to Florida. We're going to be at Doral because I'm making a speech there the following day for a group — a very important group. And then, I guess we come back to Washington. So, we're heading, as you know, to Miami — Doral.

Okay. Any questions?

Q Are you going to get a round of golf in?

THE PRESIDENT: No, I don't think so. It's so busy.

Q What's your favorite part on the plane, Mr. President? What do you like — you know?

THE PRESIDENT: Which plane?

Q Like, this one. Air Force One. When you were back, what did you like —

THE PRESIDENT: The plane? No, I've been on the plane many, many times, as you know. It's a great plane. It's a special plane.

Q Do you still want to change the colors?

THE PRESIDENT: Who?

Q Do you still want to change the colors — the exterior?

THE PRESIDENT: I would change them. Sure. It'd be a much more appropriate plane, rather than the baby blue. We want power blue, not baby blue. But no, you know, this is nice, but everything has its time and place. We'll be changing the colors.

Q Can you talk to us about the firing of the inspectors general? Why did you do that? And is it the —

THE PRESIDENT: Because it's a very common thing to do. And not all of them. Michael Horowitz, we're keeping. I thought his report on Comey was incredible, actually. It was such an accurate, well-done report. I only wish Bill Barr used it, which he chose not to. But it was — it was an incredible report. Michael Horowitz wrote the definitive report on James Comey and the FBI. It really got that going.

And I understand. I don't know them, but some people thought that some were unfair or some were not doing the job. And it's a very standard thing to do, very much like the U.S. attorneys.

Q Do you plan to bring your own people in those positions, Mr. President?

THE PRESIDENT: Which people?

Q The — in the — in the inspectors general role?

THE PRESIDENT: It's not my people. They're not my people. I don't know anybody that would do that, but we'll put people in there that will be very good.

Q Mr. President, there's reports that Elon Musk now must go through Susie Wiles and that he doesn't have an office in the West Wing. I'm curious if —

how you feel about that.

THE PRESIDENT: No, no, not — it's not Elon's office. We have an office that's set up for purposes of — when I do an executive order, that the order is carried out, not that it sits around for three months. And we'll have about 20 people, maybe more, working out of that office. It's really an office for a lot of people that go and make sure that the executive office —

You know, when I do an executive document, very important executive do- — I want to make sure that that is done. And there's about 20 or 25 people that will be working out of that office, and it's really a "go get 'em" office to make sure it gets done. That's what that is.

Q So, you're a week in now to your presidency. How does it compare to your first week in 2017? Did you learn any lessons or are you trying to do something differently?

THE PRESIDENT: Well, I come in now with great knowledge and experience and you could say that no — if you call it "new president" has ever had this kind of experience, that's for sure. Whereas before, I had never done it before, but we did well.

We had a very — we had a great presidency, but this one could be really outstanding. I think you're seeing the same reports that I see. And you write the reports. Most of you are writing the important reports. We're getting A-pluses on the work done and also the amount of work done. I mean, nobody else has done this.

You go to North Carolina. Then you go to Los Angeles. And then you stop on the way home and — and that was "no tax on tips," but it was really a stop to thank the people of Nevada for having been — you know, it's a very hard state to win as a — as a Republican, and we won it very conclusively. So, it was really more of a thank you to the people of Nevada. So, I stopped there. And I have a lot of meetings once I get back, once I get to Miami.

But no, it's — I think we had — people are saying it was the most successful first week that anybody can remember a president having.

Q Mr. President, you were so nice to Governor Newsom yesterday. No "News-" — you know, "Governor Newscum." What was that about?

THE PRESIDENT: I decided to be nice. It was nice that he came to the plane, honestly. You know, I didn't know he'd be at the plane. It was nice that he came to the plane.

And in the end, you know, we have the same goal. We want to make — take that catastrophe and make it as good as possible.

We disagree in some things. I guess he's not so set on water, and I like water for putting out fires. I find it to be extremely good. Very — a little old fashioned, but about the best thing that God has ever created for putting out fires.

And so, we're going to be doing something on that. But no, I get along — I actually always got along with him well until fairly recently.

Q If I could ask you about the first lady —

THE PRESIDENT: And I very much — you know, I very much predicted that was going to happen. Because if you go back, like, six years, I said, "If you don't start getting this place taken care of and mitigating some of the problems that are here, you're going to end up with a fire like you had ever seen." I turned out to be right.

Q If I could ask you about the first lady. She seems to be taking a more public-facing role. I just wonder how you envision her spending the next four years.

THE PRESIDENT: Well, I think she was always very much involved, but you didn't see her — more behind the scenes. But she was always a "front of the scenes" person, and I think she really wanted — she felt badly about North Carolina, and she felt very badly about California. Los Angeles — got a lot of friends. I have a lot of friends in North Carolina and — and both. And she has a lot of friends in California.

So, she wanted to be with me for that. Yeah. For

both of them.

Q Mr. President, is your preference for Larry Ellison to work to obtain TikTok? Or do you have any preference on how this deal is going?

THE PRESIDENT: I haven't spoken — Larry is a friend of mine. Lives in — you know, right in — near Mar-a-Lago, right down the road. I never spoke to Larry about TikTok.

Q But there is —

THE PRESIDENT: I've spoken to many people about TikTok, and there's great interest in TikTok. And as you know, I have the right to sell it or close it, depending on what I think is best for the country.

So, we'll make a decision over the next 90 days or so.

Q There is a report, Mr. President, that says that you are putting together a deal with Oracle and outside investors to help them buy TikTok and save TikTok. Is that happening?

THE PRESIDENT: No, not with Oracle. With — numerous people are talking to me — very substantial people — about buying it. And I'd make that decision over the next — probably over the next 30 days.

I have 90 days. Congress has given 90 days, and we'll see. If we could save TikTok, I think it would be a good thing.

So, we'll make a decision. We have a lot of interest in it. And the United States will be a big beneficiary if we do it. I'd only do it if the United States benefits.

I mean, I have a warm spot in my heart for TikTok because I won on TikTok — and I ended up winning by a lot — young people. And as you know, Republicans historically — I don't think — ever won young people, and I won them by a lot. So, I do have a little bit of a warm spot.

But, you know, it's a very popular site, and the kids are loving it, and some of the parents are loving it. And if we can save it, I think that would be a very good thing. And I think it would be economically good for America.

Q Mr. President, could I ask you about Ukraine? Do you have any update on when you are going to talk to Russian president Vad- — Russian President Putin?

THE PRESIDENT: He wants to speak, and we'll be speaking soon. And I've spoken to President Zelenskyy numerous times, and they'd like to see peace. They would like to see an end to the war. And I think President Putin would like to see an end to the war too. So, we'll see if we can help it along.

Q On the —

THE PRESIDENT: I think it's a shame. It's a war

that would have never happened if I were president. It's a shame.

Q We've seen a lot of people being fired from the federal government. What's the sort of criterion you're using for this? Is it loyalty to you? And can we expect more of these purges?

THE PRESIDENT: You have to show up to work, basically. You have to show up to work. You have to go to your office, and you have to work. And otherwise, you're not going to have a job.

Q Do you worry that that limits the pool of talent?

THE PRESIDENT: No, I think the talent is deep. We have very deep talent. But we also have a lot of excess people. You know, this was just a — this was a gimmick for Democrats, to a certain extent. But we have a lot of excess people, but the talent is very deep.

Q Now that you've done your first domestic trip, have you given any thought to where you want to go for your first international trip?

THE PRESIDENT: Well, it could be Saudi Arabia. It could be UK. Traditionally, it's been UK. Last time, I went to Saudi Arabia because they agreed to buy 450 billion dollars' worth of United States merchandise, including a lot of military equipment and farm equipment and other equipment. And if that offer were right, I'd do that again.

Q If you go to the UK, do you think you'll get

along with Keir Starmer and the Labor government?

THE PRESIDENT: I do. I mean, I've met him already three times. He's come over to see me twice. I have a call — he and I have a call over the next 24 hours.

No, I get along with him well. I like him a lot. He's liberal, which is a little bit different for me. But I think he's a very good person. I think he's — he's done a very good job thus far. He's very new on the job, but he's represented his country in terms of his philosophy. I may not agree with his philosophy, but I have a very good relationship with him. I've seen him twice. Had dinner with him at Trump Tower, as you probably know. You know that, right?

Q Just on Saudi, Mr. President. You spoke to the crown prince. Did you discuss a normalization deal between Israel and Saudi?

THE PRESIDENT: No, I discussed getting oil prices down. Because if you get oil prices down, Russia will stop the war, and Biden should have never allowed them to go up so high.

When Biden let them go up to that level, he was just inducing Russia, which sells oil, to go into a war. So, he should have never allowed — the Democrats, namely Biden, allowed oil prices to go up. That's one of the reasons that you have the Ukraine catastrophe.

Q How do you bring the prices down?

THE PRESIDENT: Volume. Yeah.

Q (Inaudible) increasing production.

THE PRESIDENT: Yeah.

Q Can you tell us about your call with the king of Jordan today, please?

THE PRESIDENT: It was a very good call. He's a friend of mine. I know him very well. I've gotten along with him over the years very well, and he's done a wonderful job.

He really houses, you know, millions of Palestinians, and he does it in a very humane way. And I compliment him on that. But he really — Jordan has done an amazing job of housing largely Palestin- — Palestinians. And he's done it in a very successful way.

Q So, what was the subject of discussion? Was it — was it —

THE PRESIDENT: It was that. I said to him, "I'd love you to take on more." Because I'm looking at the whole Gaza Strip right now, and it's a mess. It's a real mess.

Q So, you'd like Jordan to house people from Gaza?

THE PRESIDENT: You have to take people. I'd like Egypt to take people. I'm meeting with — I'm talking to General el-Sisi tomorrow — sometime, I believe. And I'd like Egypt to take people, and I'd like Jordan to take people.

I can — I mean, you're talking about probably a

million and a half people, and we just clean out that whole thing. It's — you know, it's — over the centuries, that's — that's many, many conflicts, that site.

And I don't know. It's something has to happen, but it's literally a demolition site right now. Almost everything is demolished, and people are dying there. So, I'd rather get involved with some of the Arab nations and build housing at a different location where they can maybe live in peace for a change.

Q Temporary? Or would they — would they ever go back?

THE PRESIDENT: It could be either. It could be temporarily, could be long term.

Q Go ahead.

Q You've spoken about artificial intelligence quite a bit this week.

THE PRESIDENT: Yeah.

Q Do you have any concerns about the risks to — to humanity about artificial superintelligence?

THE PRESIDENT: Well, look, artificial intelligence is the — it's where all of the smart countries want to be going. Great for coming up with cures to disease, great with coming up with everything, but there are always risks.

And it's the first question I ask: How do you absolve yourself from (inaudible), et cetera? Because it could be the rabbit that gets away. We're not going to let that happen.

But it's going to be the biggest field — maybe the biggest field in the world, and we're going to be equipped to take it. And we're already leading. I mean, we're going to be leading. Very shortly, we're going to be leading by a lot.

What they do need is tremendous energy. They need electricity at levels that nobody has ever seen before, and we'll be able to supply that electric. I'm going to use —

Q The Pentagon —

THE PRESIDENT: I'll be using emergency power to give that electric.

Q The Pentagon, Mr. President, just lifted a hold on 2,000-pound bombs for Israel, which was blocked by Biden. Can you — do you have a comment on that, sir?

THE PRESIDENT: On the what?

Q On the 2,000-pound bombs —

THE PRESIDENT: Oh.

Q — that Biden had put a hold on.

THE PRESIDENT: We released them.

Q Yeah.

THE PRESIDENT: We released them today, and they'll have them, and they paid for them, and, you know, they've been waiting for them for a long time. They've been in storage for a long time.

But we released them today to Israel.

Q Why did you do that, sir?

THE PRESIDENT: Because they bought them.

Q There are reports, Mr. President, that you spoke to the Danish prime minister and she told you Greenland is not for sale. Will you take no for an answer on that?

THE PRESIDENT: Who are you with?

Q CNN.

THE PRESIDENT: Oh.

Q (Laughs.) Your favorite.

THE PRESIDENT: No, they're terrible. Honestly, that's why they're going out of business. It's terrible. Or they'll be bought cheap. Maybe some rich guy will buy them cheap. But anyway, it's just the tone of your question every time.

I think Greenland will be worked out with us. I think we're going to have it. And I think the people want to be with us, as you know. There's 55,000 people there. They want to be with us.

I don't know, really, what claim Denmark has to it, but it would be a very unfriendly act if they didn't allow that to happen. Because that's for protection of the free world. It's not for us; it's for the free world.

Right now, you have Russian ships. You have China ships. You have ships from various countries. It's not a good situation.

And I believe we'll get that. Yeah, I do believe it. I think we'll get other things too that you're talking about, that nobody knows. But I think we'll get other — other things.

But I do believe Greenland we'll get, because it really has to do with freedom of the world, not just freedom of — it has nothing to do with the United States, other than we're the one that can provide the freedom. They can't. They can't.

I mean, they put two dog sleds there two weeks ago. They thought that was protection.

Q But the other thing is Canada —

THE PRESIDENT: And you know what? The people don't like the way they've been treated by Denmark. They don't like the way they've been treated by Denmark. And they do like us.

Q Mr. President, on the Senate confirmations, Senator Vice President JD Vance had to come and — to pass the tiebreaking vote. I'm curious if you're concerned at all about any of the other nominees.

THE PRESIDENT: No. Whatever it is, it is. I think they're doing well. I think we just had a big — a big win today, as you know. Kristi Noem, I think, will be outstanding at Homeland.

And we have some other ones going. And no, I don't — you know, I don't see any major problems.

Q The U.S. — the U.S. has suspended most foreign aid, including PEPFAR, which is a program that's credited with saving millions of lives in Africa. Is there a timeline for opening up U.S. aid? Is there a review —

THE PRESIDENT: We'll see — we'll see about that. But we want other people to join us, because we're like a one-way street. So, we want other people to help us, and we want other people to join us.

We're spending billions and billions and billions of dollars, and other countries that are wealthy are spending zero. And we want them to help. Why should we be the only one? So, they understand that. They've been told that.

It's a little like NATO. I mean, we were spending — we were almost paying for all of NATO. And yet, they were taking advantage of us on trade. Similar countries. The same and similar countries.

And after I got involved, they were paying a lot of money on NATO. The Secretary General was very generous in his statements about me with respect to NATO.

So, we'll see. I think NATO should be more too, though. I think it should be more than the two. It should be — should be five, actually.

Q The CIA, Mr. President, prefers to — prefers the lab leak theory to explain COVID's origins now. I was curious to hear your thoughts on that.

THE PRESIDENT: Well, you have a good man there. A very good man. And John is — he's just gotten approved, as you know. John Ratcliffe also got approved. And I'd rather have you ask him that question.

He'll be — he knows everything about it right now.

Q Have you had a chance — have you given any thought to the future of the air base at Diego Garcia, which, as you know, is part of the Chagos Islands, which Britain is returning to the Mauritius islands. There are concerns that could open it up to spying by Iran or China. Do you have —

THE PRESIDENT: I mean, it hasn't been number one on my list, I'll be honest with you. That was not number one.

Q (Inaudible) you didn't talk about Canada, about the Panama Canal. You mentioned today expansion

THE PRESIDENT: I think Canada has been treating us very unfairly on trade, and they've taken advantage of us for years, and we're not going to allow that to happen.

I love Canada. I have so many friends up in Canada, and they like us and they like me. But Canada has been taking advantage of the United States for years, and we're not going to let that happen.

And without our subsidy, Canada, you know, doesn't exist really. It's very — it's — Canada is totally reliant on us, therefore they should be a state. Canada — we lose $250 billion a year on Canada. I could stop that in one day. And if I stopped that, Canada wouldn't exist as a state, you know, as a — as a country.

And I think if that's going to — if we're going to have to give that kind of subsidy — and we're not even talking about tariffs yet, but that'll happen on February 1st.

But if we're going to lose $250 billion for the sake of supporting a country, it's not fair to us. And they do about almost 90 percent of their business with the United States, whereas with us, it's the opposite. It's, you know, relatively small.

So, I don't want to spend hundreds of billions of dollars on supporting a country unless that country is a state. And if it is a state, the people of Canada would pay a much lower tax. You know, their taxes would be cut in half. They would have no military problems. They'd be much more secure in every way.

And I think it's a great thing for Canada. And I view it as, you know, honestly, a country that should be a state, and they'll get much better treatment, much better care, and much lower taxes, and they'll be much more secure.

Thank you very much, everybody.

Q Thank you for coming back.

THE PRESIDENT: Thank you.

www.ingramcontent.com/pod-product-compliance
Lightning Source LLC
LaVergne TN
LVHW040520210926
848480LV00007BA/1528
*9798348487942*